PLAYH

A West Yorkshire Playhouse production

(the fall of)
THE MASTER BUILDER

by ZINNIE HARRIS
after Ibsen

This production of
(the fall of) The Master Builder
was first performed at West Yorkshire Playhouse
on 30 September 2017.

Cast

ALINE	Susan Cookson
HALVARD SOLNESS	Reece Dinsdale
DR HERDAL	David Hounslow
HILDE	Katherine Rose Morley
KAJA	Emma Naomi
RAGNAR	Michael Peavoy
BROVIK	Robert Pickavance

Creative Team

Writer	Zinnie Harris
Director	James Brining
Designer	Alex Lowde
Lighting Designer	Sinéad McKenna
Sound Designer	Jon Nicholls
Assistant Director (*Birkbeck*)	Laurence Young
Trainee Assistant Director	Callum Mardy
Casting Director	Ginny Schiller CDG

Production

Company Stage Manager	Richard Pattison
Stage Manager	Julie Issott
Deputy Stage Manager	Richard Lodge
Assistant Stage Manager	Lucy Bradford

Cast Biographies

Susan Cookson | Aline

Theatre credits include: *Romeo and Juliet*, *Beryl* (West Yorkshire Playhouse); *Losing the Plot* (Theatre Royal Windsor/No 1 Tour); *Jack Steele and Family* (Crucible Theatre); *The Man with Everything* (Royal Exchange); *April in Paris*, *Can't Stand Up for Falling Down*, *Passion Killers*, *Two* (Hull Truck); *Dick Whittington*, *Playboy of the Western World* (Oldham Coliseum), *Shakers* (Wolsey Theatre); *Up 'n Under* (York Theatre Royal). Her television credits include: *Hollyoaks*, *Cold Feet*, *DCI Banks*, *Coronation Street*, *Doctors*, *After Hours*, *Casualty*, *Last Tango in Halifax*, *Mount Pleasant*, *Secret State*, *More Than Words*, *Land Girls*, *The Borgias*, *Waterloo Road*, *Five Days*, *Moving On*, *Bodies*, *Early Doors*, *The Royal*, *Blue Murder*, *Emmerdale*, *Mersey Beat*, *Clocking Off*, *Shipman*, *Fat Friends*, *Queer as Folk*, *The Innocent*, *How to Do Love in the Twenty-First Century*, *City Central*, *Heartbeat*, *Into the Fire*, *Peak Practice*. Her film credits include: *Raining Stones*. Her radio credits include: *The Best Queue*, *A Little Happiness*, *The Kansas to Deptford*, *Millionaires*, *Brave Swimmers*, *Stake Out*, *South Riding*, *The Drought*.

Reece Dinsdale | Halvard Solness

Theatre Credits include: *This House*, *Racing Demon* (National Theatre); *Wild Oats*, *The Playboy of the Western World*, *The Revenger's Tragedy*, *Visiting Mr Green*, *Untold Stories* and *Richard III* (West Yorkshire Playhouse); *Absence of War* (Headlong); *Woundings*, *Don Carlos* and *The Lady From The Sea* (Royal Exchange, Manchester); *Love You, Too* and *Boys Mean Business* (Bush Theatre); *Mirandolina* (Lyric Hammersmith); *Observe the Sons of Ulster Marching Towards the Somme*, *A Going Concern* and *Morning and Evening* (Hampstead Theatre); *Rhinoceros* (Nuffield Theatre); *Old Year's Eve* (RSC); *Beethoven's Tenth* (Vaudeville, West End); *Red Saturday* (Royal Court).

Film includes: *Hamlet*; *ID* (Special Jury Prize for Best Actor – Geneva Film Festival); *A Private Function*; *Rabbit on the Moon*; *Romance and Rejection*; *The Knife That Killed Me*; *Acid Burn* (short); *China* (short).

Television includes: *Silent Witness*; *Moving On*; *Midnight Man*; *Life on Mars*; *Dalziel and Pascoe*; *The Chase*; *Love Lies Bleeding*; *Ahead of the Class*; *Conviction*; *The Trouble With George*; *Spooks*; *Born and Bred*; *The*

Investigation; In Deep; Taggart; Waterloo Road; Coronation Street; Murder in Mind; Bliss; Thief Takers; Lovejoy; Full Stretch; Young Catherine; Haggard; The Attractions; Take me Home; Coppers; The Storyteller; Bergerac; Home to Roost; Robin of Sherwood; Glamour Night; Winter Fight; Threads; Partners in Crime; The Secret Adversary; Out On The Floor; Knife Edge.

As Director (for television) credits include: 'The Crossing' for *Secrets and Words* (BBC1) and 'Madge', 'Scratch', and 'Eighteen' for *Moving On* (BBC1).

As Writer his credits include: *Imaginary Friend* (short film).

David Hounslow | Dr Herdal

Theatre credits include: *The Snowman* (Leicester Haymarket); *Othello* (RSC); *Bent* (National Theatre); *Treasure Island* (Farnham Redgrave); *Billy Budd* (Sheffield Crucible); *Fuente Ovejuna* (National Theatre); *Our Boys* (Cockpit Theatre); *Henry V, Coriolanus, The Wives' Excuse* and *Zenobia* (all for the RSC), *All of You Mine* (Bush Theatre); *Perpetua* (Birmingham Rep); *Alcestis* (Northern Broadsides); *Tales from Hollywood* and *Privates on Parade* (Donmar Warehouse); *My Night with Reg* and *Dealer's Choice* (Birmingham Repertory Theatre); *Holes In The Skin* (Chichester Festival Theatre); *The Rise and Fall of Little Voice* (Manchester Royal Exchange); *A Night at the Dogs* (Soho Theatre); *Tamburlaine* (Bristol Old Vic); *Billy Liar* (Liverpool Playhouse). More recently David has appeared in *Warm* (Theatre 503); *First Person Shooter* (Birmingham Rep); *Too Much Pressure* (Belgrade Theatre); *Way Upstream* (Salisbury Playhouse); *Macbeth* (Sheffield Crucible); *This House* (National Theatre); *The Empty Quarter* (Hampstead Theatre Downstairs); *Queen Coal* (Sheffield Crucible); *This House* (Chichester Festival Theatre and Garrick Theatre, West End).

Television credits include: *The Unknown Soldier, True Blues, Othello, Children of the North, Gone to the Dogs, Resnick, True Crimes, Minder, Bad Company, Under The Hammer, Anna Lee, Soldier Soldier, Deadly Crack, The Cinder Path, Chandler and Co., Six Sides of Coogan, Crimes and Punishment, Turning World, Is It Legal, Peak Practice, A Wing and a Prayer, Dangerfield, Playing the Field, The Unknown Soldier, Bugs, Crimewatch, Within Living Memory, Casualty, Eastenders, City Central, Bomber, Always and Everyone, Other People's Children, Peak Practice, Silent Witness, North Square, Casualty, London's Burning, Margery & Gladys, Eastenders, The Bill, Ultimate Force, Heartbeat and Crisis Command, Blackpool, Holby City, The Brief, Doctors,*

Robin Hood, Jekyll, Dalziel And Pascoe, Is This Love?, Coronation Street, Little Miss Jocelyn, MI High, Dead Set, Bonekickers, Waking The Dead, Spooks IX, Homefront, Foyle's War, The Bletchley Circle II, Emmerdale, Moving On and *Bad Move*.

Film credits include: *London Kills Me, Captives, Fever Pitch, The Man Who Knew Too Little, I Want You, Tabloid TV, The Flying Scotsman, The International, Defining Fay, Ginger and Rosa, Peterloo*.

Radio credits include: numerous radio plays for BBC Radio, including being a member of the BBC Repertory Company.

Katherine Rose Morley | Hilde

Katherine Rose Morley trained at the Guildhall School of Music and Drama.

Theatre credits include: *Once a Catholic* (Tricycle Theatre/Royal Court Liverpool); *Khadija is 18* (Finborough Theatre).

Her TV credits include *Last Tango in Halifax – Christmas Special* (Red Productions for BBC One); *Thirteen* (BBC); *Call the Midwife* (Neal Street Productions for BBC1); *Moving On* (LA Productions for BBC1); *Cuffs* (Tiger Aspect for BBC1), *Vera* (ITV Productions for ITV1); *Fishbowl* (Bwark for BBC3); *Last Tango in Halifax* (Red Productions for ITV); *The Mill* (Series I & II) (Darlow Smithson Productions for Ch4); *Thirty and Counting* (Bwark Productions for Sky Living); *The Week Before Christmas (Sharon Horgan's Little Cracker)* (Sky1).

Emma Naomi | Kaja

Emma Naomi trained at the Guildhall School of Music and Drama.

Theatre credits include: *Dead Don't Floss* (National Theatre); *Don Juan In Soho* (Wyndhams Theatre); *Deathwatch* (Print Room at The Coronet); *The Crucible* (Bristol Old Vic); *This Man Right Here* (Hen & Chickens). Her feature film credit includes: *House Girl* (dir. Koby Adom).

Her credits while training include: *Medea, The Comedy of Errors, Burnt by The Sun, Twelfth Night, Uncle Vanya, Flare Path*.

Michael Peavoy | Ragnar

Michael Peavoy trained at the Royal Academy of Dramatic Art.

Theatre credits include: *The Railway Children* (Octagon Theatre); *Being Amazing/First Words* (Octagon Theatre); *The Tenant of Wildfell Hall* (Octagon Theatre Bolton and York Theatre Royal); *Into the Woods* (Royal Exchange); *Sweeney Todd* (West Yorkshire Playhouse /Manchester Royal Exchange); *Billy Elliott* (The Forum); *Hamlet* (National Theatre); *Broadway to West End* (Theatre Royal Drury Lane); *A Life of the Mind* (RADA); *Measure for Measure* (RADA).

Television credits include: *Musketeers* (BBC); *The Five* (Red Productions); *Our World War* (BBC); *Lewis* (ITV); *Doctors* (BBC); *Casualty* (BBC)

Robert Pickavance | Brovik

At West Yorkshire Playhouse: *James and the Giant Peach, The Market, Mela, Huddersfield, Coming Around Again, Foe* (co-production with Complicite), *What Every Woman Knows* and *The Pope And The Witch*. Recent theatre credits include: *The Twits* (Leicester Curve); *Much Ado About Nothing* (Shakespeare's Globe on tour); *The Grand Gesture* and *The Canterbury Tales* (Northern Broadsides); *40 Years On, Peter Pan, The Wind In The Willows, The Homecoming, The White Crow, Patient No 1, The Hare And The Tortoise, The Dumb Waiter, Pygmalion, Broken Glass, Walking The Tightrope, Hobson's Choice, Macbeth, Bedtime Stories, Neville's Island, Educating Rita, Romeo and Juliet* (York Theatre Royal); *The BFG, Dracula, What The Butler Saw, The Railway Children, Who's Afraid of Virginia Woolf?* and *Two-Way Mirror* (Duke's Theatre, Lancaster); *Oliver Twist, A Christmas Carol* and *Anna Karenina* (Bolton Octagon); *When We Dead Awaken* (Vasterbottensteatern, Sweden). With Gerry Mulgrew and Alison Peebles, Rob co-founded the Scottish company Communicado in Edinburgh, appearing in 14 of their productions, including *Tales from the Arabian Nights, Cyrano de Bergerac* and Jock Tamson's *Bairns and Carmen*.

Television includes: *Midsomer Murders, A Touch of Frost, Foyle's War, Gas Attack, Kavanagh QC, City Central, The Colour of Light* and, for German TV, *Die Betrogene*.

He has also performed in concerts with the Halle Orchestra, most recently in a BBC Prom at the Albert Hall in August 2017.

Film credits include: *Caravan* (The Uprising Features Ltd). Radio credits include: *Pride and Prejudice* (BBC Radio 4), *Singles Going Steady* (BBC); *Inappropriate Relationships* (BBC).

Creative Biographies

Zinnie Harris | Writer

Zinnie Harris is a playwright, screenwriter and theatre director. In summer 2017 her new play *Meet Me at Dawn* premiered at the Traverse Theatre, while her new adaptation of Ionesco's *Rhinoceros* and a revival of her trilogy *This Restless House* opened as part of the Edinburgh International Festival. *This Restless House*, which first premiered at the Citizens Theatre, Glasgow in 2016, was winner of Best New Play at the Critics' Awards for Theatre in Scotland 2016 and shortlisted for the Susan Smith Blackburn Prize 2016/17. Other plays include *How to Hold Your Breath* (Royal Court Theatre), winner of the Berwin Lee Award 2015; *The Message on the Watch* (Tricycle Theatre); *The Wheel* (National Theatre of Scotland), joint winner of the 2011 Amnesty International Freedom of Expression Award and a Fringe First award; *The Panel* (Tricycle Theatre); *The Garden* (Traverse Theatre); *Fall* (Traverse Theatre); *Solstice* (RSC); *Midwinter* (RSC), winner of an Arts Foundation Fellowship Award for playwriting; *Nightingale and Chase* (Royal Court); *Further Than the Furthest Thing* (National Theatre/Tron Theatre), winner of the Peggy Ramsay Playwriting Award, the John Whiting Award and a Fringe First award; and *By Many Wounds* (Hampstead Theatre). Other adaptations include *A Doll's House* (Donmar Warehouse) and *Miss Julie* (National Theatre of Scotland).

Zinnie has also written for television and radio, with two ninety-minute dramas for Channel 4 called *Born with Two Mothers* and *Richard Is My Boyfriend* and episodes for the BBC One drama series *Spooks*. She was lead writer on the series *Partners in Crime* (Endor/BBC 1), based on the Agatha Christie novels *Tommy and Tuppence*.

Zinnie is currently under commission to the Royal Court, the Royal Shakespeare Company and the Royal National Theatre. She has been Associate Director at the Traverse Theatre since spring 2015 and is Professor of Playwriting and Screenwriting at St Andrews University.

James Brining

Director / Joint CEO of West Yorkshire Playhouse

James Brining was born and brought up in Leeds.

After studying English at University, James ran his own theatre company in Newcastle upon Tyne on the Enterprise Allowance Scheme. He subsequently became Artistic Director of Proteus Theatre Company, a new writing company touring community venues and small theatres around the South of England. He then moved to the Orange Tree Theatre in Richmond where he was Community Director.

In 1997 James moved to Glasgow to take up the post of Artistic Director of TAG Theatre Company, Scotland's national theatre for children and young people. In 1999 he launched a four-year drama and democracy project, *Making the Nation*, which explored devolution and independence on both national and international platforms through plays and innovative participation projects. He commissioned and directed new pieces by writers including David Greig, Edwin Morgan, Sarah Woods, John McGrath and Stephen Greenhorn. TAG shows were performed throughout Scotland, in theatres, schools, community venues, prisons and found spaces including the new Scottish Parliament as well as touring to Japan, Europe and North America. Whilst at TAG he also directed site-specific work, radio drama for the BBC and two productions at LIFT.

In 2003 he was appointed Artistic Director/Chief Executive of Dundee Rep Theatre, where James directed new and classic work including: *Further Than the Furthest Thing*, *A Christmas Carol*, *Who's Afraid of Virginia Woolf?*, *Romeo and Juliet*, *The Firebird*, *Sweet Bird of Youth*, *Gypsy*, *Flora the Red Menace*, *A Lie of the Mind*, *Dr Korczak's Example* and *Cinderella*. He significantly expanded the Rep's creative learning activities, pioneering a range of artist development and dramatherapy programmes and a significant expansion of the youth theatres. He founded a new MA in Theatre Studies jointly taught with the University of Dundee and was Chairman of the Federation of Scottish Theatre, the membership body for Scotland's theatres and theatre companies.

Since joining West Yorkshire Playhouse as Artistic Director and Joint CEO, James has directed *Into the Woods* in a co-production with Opera North, *Chitty Chitty Bang Bang*, *The Rise and Fall of Little Voice*, *The Crucible*, *Enjoy*, *Talking Heads* and *Sweeney Todd: The Demon Barber of Fleet Street*. He re-created *Sweeney Todd* for Welsh National Opera at Wales Millennium Centre and on tour as well as restaging the show in Brussels for La Monnaie, Belgium's national opera company. His most recent production was Zodwa Nyoni's new play, *Ode to Leeds*.

Alex Lowde | Designer

Alex read Drama at Hull University before training in design at Motley.

Theatre includes: *August: Osage County* (Dundee Rep; *Persuasion* (Manchester Royal Exchange); *Pygmalion* (Headlong, West Yorkshire Playhouse and Nuffield Southampton); *Three Sisters* (Lyric Belfast); *Dedication* (Nuffield Theatre, Southampton); *Dutchman* (Young Vic Theatre); *Linda* (Royal Court); *Lines* (The Yard); *Miss Julie* (Aarhus Theatre); *Game* (Almeida); *Stink Foot* (The Yard); *'Tis Pity She's a Whore* (Shakespeare's Globe); *Krapp's Last Tape* (Sheffield Theatre); *Enjoy* (West Yorkshire Playhouse); *The Body of an American* (The Gate); *Edward II* (National Theatre); *A Christmas Carol, Takin' over the Asylum, The Marriage of Figaro* (Edinburgh Lyceum); *Innocence* (Scottish Dance Theatre); *Carousel* (Royal Conservatoire of Scotland); *Blake Diptych* (Laban); *Victoria Station/One for the Road* (The Young Vic/Print Room); *A Clockwork Orange* (Stratford East); *While You Lie* (Traverse);*The Glass Menagerie, Anna Karenina, Beauty and the Beast, She Town, A Doll's House, The Elephant Man, Equus* (Dundee Rep).

Opera includes: *Greek* (Edinburgh International Theatre, Scottish Opera); *Rigoletto* (Opera Theatre Company Wexford, UK tour); *The Adventures of Mr Broucek* (Opera North and Scottish Opera); *Tobias and the Angel* (Young Vic); *The Lion's Face, The Nose* (ROH2/The Opera Group); *Paradise Moscow* (Royal Academy of Music); *The Gentle Giant* (ROH education); *Le Nozze di Figaro* (Sadler's Wells).

Sinéad McKenna | Lighting Designer

Sinéad has received two Irish Times Theatre Awards for Best Lighting Design.

Recent designs include *Grace Jones– Bloodlight* and *Bami* (Blinder Films); *Angela's Ashes: The Musical; Futureproof* (Cork Everyman Palace); *Nivellis War* (Cahoots NI/ New Victory Theatre Broadway).

Other designs include The Becket/Pinter/Friel Festival, Private Lives (2016 and 2008); *Juno and the Paycock, A Month in the Country, The Gigli Concert, The Mariner, The Price and An Ideal Husband* (The Gate Theatre); *Maz and Bricks* (Fishamble); *The Wake, Othello, Aristocrats, Quietly, Alice in Funderland, The Plough and the Stars, 16 Possible Glimpses, The Burial at Thebes, Howie the Rookie, Finders Keepers* (Abbey Theatre); *New Electric Ballroom* (Druid); *Howie the Rookie, Greener, October, Last Days of the Celtic Tiger, Blackbird* (Landmark Productions); *Dubliners* (The Corn Exchange); *Famished Castle, Travesties, The Importance of Being Earnest, Improbable Frequency* (Drama Desk nomination 2009 Best Lighting Design for a Musical), *The Parker Project, Life is a Dream, Attempts on her Life, Dream of Autumn* (Rough Magic); *The Wolf and Peter, Agnes, Pageant, Swept* (Cois Ceim); *Invitation to a journey* (Coisceim/Fishamble/Crash Ensemble); *Don Giovanni* (OTC); *La Traviata* (Malmo Opera House); *The Rape of Lucretia, The Magic*

Flute, *The Marriage of Figaro* (Opera Theatre Company); and *Midsummers Night Dream* (Opera Ireland).

She has also worked with Decadent, Gar San Lazare, Corn Exchange, THISISPOPBABY, Siren, The Lyric, Second Age, Performance Corporation, Semper Fi and Guna Nua.

Jon Nicholls | Sound Designer

Jon Nicholls studied composition at the London College of Music and electroacoustic music at Dartington.

Music/sound scores for theatre include: *Hamlet* (RSC); *Spring Storm*, *Beyond The Horizon* and *The Holy Rosenbergs* (National Theatre); *Good Canary*, *My Brilliant Friend* (Rose); *Bakersfield Mist* (Duchess); *Yerma*, *Idomeneus* (Gate); *Bracken Moor*, *Mermaid* (Shared Experience); *Pink Mist*, *Medea* (Bristol Old Vic); *The Duchess Of Malfi*, *The Revenger's Tragedy* (Nottingham Playhouse); *Richard III* (West Yorkshire Playhouse); *Who's Afraid of Virginia Woolf?* (Sheffield Crucible); *The Norman Conquests* (Liverpool Playhouse); *The Mother*, *Things We Do for Love*, *Trouble in Mind* (Bath Theatre Royal); and many other productions for theatres including Leicester Curve, Northampton Royal & Derngate, Northern Stage, Bath Ustinov Studio, Birmingham Rep, Theatr Clwyd, & Salisbury Playhouse.

Screen work includes: scores for numerous documentaries for the BBC, ITV, Channel 4, Sky and Al Jazeera, and over 30 short films. He has also created music and sound design for over 20 BBC radio dramas, and composed two operas, most recently *Flicker*, premiered at Sadlers Wells with Aurora Orchestra. He's currently working with the Society of Strange & Ancient Instruments on *soundhouse*, a national touring project combining seventeenth-century instruments with live electronics inspired by the writings of Francis Bacon.

Laurence Young | Assistant Director (Birkbeck)

Laurence is currently training on the MFA Theatre Directing programme at Birkbeck University, London, and is on attachment at the West Yorkshire Playhouse as Trainee Director. (*the fall of) The Master Builder* is his first show Assistant Director at the Playhouse, and he will soon be assisting Sally Cookson on *The Lion, The Witch, and The Wardrobe*.

Prior to joining the Playhouse he studied Anthropology at University College London, where he directed many productions including *Constellations* (by Nick Payne) and an original devised version of Lewis Carroll's *The Jabberwocky*. Laurence also trained on the FdA Acting course at Bristol Old Vic Theatre School.

Callum Mardy | Trainee Assistant Director

Callum Mardy is in his final year of an Acting course at Leeds City College. He has been very involved with the West Yorkshire Playhouse's First Floor for almost five years, during which time he took part in four performances for NT Connections, several of First Floor's Showcases and three performances for the Light Night Festival. He has also toured with First Floor around Leeds as part of the Kes project and was involved in the companion piece that came with it. Most recently, he has worked with the Playhouse's Associate Director Amy Leach as part of the young company for *Romeo and Juliet* (West Yorkshire Playhouse).

Ginny Schiller CDG | Casting Director

Ginny Schiller has been an in-house casting director for the Royal Shakespeare Company, Chichester Festival Theatre, Rose Theatre Kingston, English Touring Theatre and Soho Theatre. She collaborates regularly with Theatre Royal Bath on their main house, touring and West End productions, and is the casting director for the Ustinov Theatre, Bath, under the artistic directorship of Laurence Boswell. She has worked on many shows for the West End and No. 1 touring circuit as well as for the Almeida, Arcola, Birmingham Rep, Bolton Octagon, Bristol Old Vic, Clwyd Theatr Cyrmu, Frantic Assembly, Greenwich Theatre, Hampstead Theatre, Headlong, Liverpool Everyman and Playhouse, Lyric Theatre Belfast, Menier Chocolate Factory, Norfolk & Norwich Festival, Northampton Royal & Derngate, Oxford Playhouse, Plymouth Theatre Royal and Drum, Regent's Park Open Air Theatre, Shared Experience, Sheffield Crucible, West Yorkshire Playhouse, Wilton's Music Hall and Young Vic. She has also worked on many television, film and radio productions.

West Yorkshire Playhouse

Welcome to the home of incredible stories

There has been a Playhouse in Leeds for almost fifty years; from 1968 to 1990 as Leeds Playhouse and then with the opening of a brand new theatre on its current Quarry Hill site it became West Yorkshire Playhouse.

West Yorkshire Playhouse is a leading UK producing theatre; a cultural hub, a place where people gather to tell and share stories and to engage in world class theatre. We make work which is pioneering and relevant, seeking out the best companies and artists to create inspirational theatre in the heart of Yorkshire. From large-scale spectacle to intimate performance we develop and make work for our stages, for found spaces, for touring, for schools and community centres. We create work to entertain and inspire.

As dedicated collaborators, we work regularly with other theatres from across the UK, independent producers, and some of the most distinctive, original voices in theatre today. We develop work with established practitioners and find, nurture and support new voices that ought to be heard. We cultivate new talent by providing creative space for new writers, emerging directors, companies and individual theatre makers to refine their practice.

Alongside our work for the stage we are dedicated to providing creative engagement opportunities that excite and stimulate. We build, run and sustain projects which reach out to everyone from refugee communities, to young people and students, to older communities and people with learning disabilities. At the Playhouse there is always a way to get involved.

West Yorkshire Playhouse – Vital Theatre

Artistic Director   James Brining
Executive Director   Robin Hawkes

Chairman of the Board   Sir Rodney Brooke CBE

Find us on Facebook: West Yorkshire Playhouse
Follow us on Twitter: @wyplayhouse
wyp.org.uk

Leeds Theatre Trust Limited   Charity Number 255460

VAT No. 545 4890 17 Company No. 926862, England Wales

Registered address Playhouse Square, Quarry Hill, Leeds, LS2 7UP

Supporters and Thanks

Major Funders

Access Partner

Production Sponsor
Crumble's Search for Christmas

Partners

Directors Club
Gold Members

Silver Members

 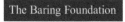

Bronze Members

Trusts and Foundations

Chadwick Charitable Trust
The Charles Brotherton Trust
The Linden Charitable Trust
Leeds Youth Activity Fund
Safer Communities Fund
Leeds Looked After Children Fund

Project Partners

Leeds Theatre Trust Limited operating as West Yorkshire Playhouse
is a not-for-profit organisationand a registered charity (number 255460).
For more information on how you could help to support the valuable work
in our theatres, local schools and communities please contact

(the fall of)
The Master Builder

ZINNIE HARRIS *after* IBSEN

Zinnie Harris's plays include the multi-award-winning *Further than the Furthest Thing* (National Theatre/Tron Theatre; winner of the 1999 Peggy Ramsay Award, 2001 John Whiting Award, Edinburgh Fringe First Award), *How to Hold Your Breath* (Royal Court Theatre; joint winner of the Berwin Lee Award), *The Wheel* (National Theatre of Scotland; joint winner of the 2011 Amnesty International Freedom of Expression Award), *Nightingale and Chase* (Royal Court Theatre), *Midwinter*, *Solstice* (both RSC), *Fall* (Traverse Theatre/RSC), *By Many Wounds* (Hampstead Theatre) and *This Restless House* (National Theatre of Scotland/Citizens Theatre; Best New Play, Critics' Award for Theatre in Scotland, 2016). Her adaptations include Ibsen's *A Doll's House* and Strindberg's *Miss Julie*d. She is Professor of Playwriting and Screenwriting at St Andrews University, and an Associate Director at the Traverse Theatre.

Henrik Ibsen (1828–1906), Norwegian poet and playwright. His earliest major plays, *Brand* (1866) and *Peer Gynt* (1867), were large-scale verse dramas, but in *Pillars of the Community* (1877), *A Doll's House* (1879), *Ghosts* (1881) and *An Enemy of the People* (1882) he explord contemporary issues. A richer understanding of the complexity of human impulses marks such later works as *The Wild Duck* (1885), *Rosmersholm* (1886), *The Lady from the Sea* (1888), *Hedda Gabler* (1890) and *The Master Builder* (1892), while imminent mortality overshadows his last great plays, *John Gabriel Borkman* (1896) and *When We Dead Awaken* (1899).

also by Zinnie Harris from Faber

BY MANY WOUNDS
FURTHER THAN THE FURTHEST THING
NIGHTINGALE AND CHASE
SOLSTICE
MIDWINTER
FALL
JULIE
(after Strindberg)
A DOLL'S HOUSE
(after Ibsen)
THE WHEEL
HOW TO HOLD YOUR BREATH
THIS RESTLESS HOUSE
MEET ME AT DAWN

ZINNIE HARRIS

(*the fall of*)
The Master Builder

after
HENRIK IBSEN

FABER & FABER

First published in 2017
by Faber and Faber Ltd
74–77 Great Russell Street
London WC1B 3DA

Typeset by Country Setting, Kingsdown, Kent CT14 8ES
Printed in England by CPI Group (UK) Ltd, Croydon CR0 4YY

A CIP record for this book
is available from the British Library

978-0-571-34502-1

2 4 6 8 10 9 7 5 3 1

Director's Note

Ibsen's *The Master Builder* has traditionally been seen as a study of an aging artist. We see Halvard Solness, having reached the peak of his powers, dealing with his decline into old age: his loss of power sexually, creatively and socially. Like most classic Ibsen plays, the activities of the past are explored and unearthed and shown to affect the present.

In (*The fall of*) *The Master Builder*, more a response to than a version of Ibsen's play, Solness is a driven, determined working-class man who has, through bullish will and hunger, gained significant advancement. He takes huge pleasure in looking down on his previously more affluent, middle-class, better educated contemporaries, some of whom he has driven out of business.

Our reaction to Ibsen's great play was to reframe its characters and events for today's audience, looking particularly at one aspect through more contemporary eyes. In the original, Halvard Solness has had a liaison ten years previously with a young woman, Hilde Wangel. In Ibsen's text, Hilde was then thirteen and Halvard, having 'kissed her, and bent her backwards', sends her away for ten years, telling her to wait for him.

The narrative trope of a powerful, sexually predatory older man is all too familiar to us today. Ibsen's hero, a man tortured by guilt and with an increasing sense of impending mortality translates easily into the contemporary figure Zinnie has created.

We wanted to examine the nature of this man's desire – the way he asserts and defines himself through his sexual relationships, his desperate weakness which is in tension with his apparent strength. As importantly, we wanted to examine the impact of his behaviour on the women involved – Hilde, Aline (his wife) and Kaia, the young assistant who, in the original play, is infatuated by Solness, an infatuation he cultivates. We were also fascinated by the collusion of others in keeping these stories secret to protect 'the greater good'.

(*The fall of*) *The Master Builder* is rooted in the same narrative arc as Ibsen's play but focuses, with Zinnie's characteristic humanity and a forensic eye, on the dark sexuality latent in the original. Ibsen's work caused scandal in his lifetime, some scripts being considered so explosively amoral that several were banned. In this revisiting, Zinnie has pulled away from the drawing rooms of nineteenth-century Norway and has charged the play with a freshly explosive fuse which makes the play speak powerfully to the here and now.

James Brining, September 2017

(The fall of) The Master Builder was first performed in the Courtyard Theatre of the West Yorkshire Playhouse on 30 September 2017. The cast, in alphabetical order, was as follows:

Aline Susan Cookson
Solness Reece Dinsdale
Dr Herdal David Hounslow
Hilde Katherine Rose Morley
Kaja Emma Naomi
Ragnar Michael Peavoy
Brovik Robert Pickavance

Director James Brining
Designer Alex Lowde
Lighting Designer Sinéad McKenna

Characters

Halvard Solness
the master builder

Aline Solness
his wife

Dr Herdal
a family doctor

Knut Brovik
assistant to Solness

Ragnar Brovik
his son

Kaja Fosli
fiancée of Ragnar

Hilde Wangel

(the fall of)
THE MASTER BUILDER

Act One

Late afternoon, early evening.

A large, open-plan architects' office. Messy.

Not just piles of paper, plan chests, computers, drawings and models but also bottles of wine, balloons, some cake that is left over. The aftermath of a party.

Brovik, an old man, is stooped and clearing up.

His son is standing beside him looking around.

Ragnar
bloody mess

Brovik
take a bag would you, get those bottles –

Beat.

The young man doesn't move.

alright don't

Ragnar
I just think –

Brovik
that's the problem with you –

Ragnar
it's the principle

Brovik
there's a principle here?

Ragnar
of course

Brovik

there's a mess, it needs picking up

Ragnar

you aren't even well

Brovik

then you do it

Beat.

The young man doesn't.

maybe it's laziness, maybe it isn't principle at all
maybe you're just a slob –

Ragnar

we should have been home a while ago, you should
have been home

Brovik

yes that's true
but this will only take –

Ragnar

just leave it, Dad

Brovik

and then what?

Ragnar

I knew it,
you don't care how this place is when you come in
tomorrow
you're scared of him

Brovik

don't be absurd
why would I be scared?

Ragnar

you've been running around all week

Brovik
    he pays us

Ragnar
    not enough

Beat.

Brovik
    I don't like it like this
    will that make you happier?
    I enjoy my work and this place –

Ragnar
    the cleaner will come in in the morning

Brovik
    we'll be in before her

Ragnar
    alright I'll ring the agency, ask her to come in earlier
        for fuck's sake Dad stop

Brovik
    no you stop

Ragnar
    bad enough that he took over your company but

Brovik
    this really bothers you?

Ragnar
    I hate to see you, picking up from his floor, yes

Brovik
    and yet I run to and from the copier for him all day
    out to get his sandwich

Ragnar
    you shouldn't do that

Brovik

if I don't, he'll ask you to do it

Beat.

I actually want a word with him
and no, I don't think it will make a difference if we
   are surrounded by this rubbish, I just don't like
   standing in it myself, or alright if you insist maybe
   it will make a bit of difference, maybe a tiny bit

Ragnar

you'll never give up, will you?

Brovik

you watch, when I have a word with him –

Ragnar

don't tell me he promised to be more reasonable?

Brovik

there is nothing unreasonable about him, if you
   knew him better –

Ragnar

can't we just go home, get some dinner?

Kaja comes in.

Kaja

I booked a taxi so if we're ready – oh

Ragnar

I know

Brovik

it won't take a minute

Kaja

should he be doing that?

Ragnar

of course he shouldn't

Kaja goes to help Brovik.

and I don't suppose it helps if I say you shouldn't either

Kaja
 I don't mind

Brovik
 don't say that, you get a torrent in your ear if you
   don't mind
 good grief, the person that doesn't mind!

Ragnar
 I didn't say that

Brovik
 the person that just gets on and does something
 heaven help us

Kaja and Brovik clear up. Ragnar scowls.

Kaja
 where is he anyway?

Brovik
 just coming I think, he was talking to a woman

Kaja
 Aline says he is off his heels

Ragnar
 do you really want to speak to him now?

Brovik
 ach it'll be fine

Ragnar
 it won't count if he can't remember anything

Kaja
 what are you talking about?

Brovik

take Kaja home, I'll be right behind

Kaja

now I feel like there *is* something going on –?

Brovik

the Lovstrand house

Kaja

I thought it was all settled

Ragnar

I saw them today

Kaja

again?

Ragnar

they want to change the contract

Kaja

and ditch him?

Brovik

they didn't quite put it like that
he doesn't know any of this yet

Kaja

but you knew?

Brovik

it was my idea

Kaja

bloody hell –

Ragnar

if you are bothered, we will say you had no part of it

Kaja

I'm engaged to you
(*To Brovik.*) and I live in your house

Ragnar

    listen –

Kaja

    when he finds out you met with them –

Brovik

    let me have a word with him

    I can smooth it over

    this is nothing compared to what we have been
        through before

Kaja

    he's going to go ballistic

Ragnar

    does that matter?

Kaja

    I wish you hadn't told me now

Brovik

    go on, the pair of you, you're shattered – go
    I'll handle it

Kaja

    how?

Brovik

    I've known him since he was ten more or less. I was
        the one with jobs to hand out and he was nothing
    that has to count for something, doesn't it?

*A man walks in: this is Halvard Solness, the Master
Builder.*

Solness

    count for what?

No one says anything.

Solness

    don't tell me there is conspiracy –

I love a conspiracy. Come on you three, lighten up
this is a party, was a party
you aren't clearing up are you?

Ragnar
I did tell him not to

Solness
Kaja, you've got your coat on
don't say you are leaving?
and oh God the wine is all
look at this Brovik, someone has stuck a cigarette
    butt in a perfectly good bottle of wine, who would
    do that?

Brovik
who knows –

Solness
is there any more –?

He picks up a bottle.

Kaja, tell me that we didn't drink –

Kaja
there is some more in the fridge

Solness
excellent girl
get yourself one, let's all have a drink

He starts to dance with Brovik, who giggles, but good-naturedly isn't all that into it.

I got Architect of the Year
Master Builder UK that is me.
Master Builder, I am the Master fucking Builder
    this year
you look so worried
don't worry, whatever it is, lighten up

Brovik
   I am light

Solness
   oh Brovik my old friend
   the universe is shining on us
   or you Ragnar, you'll dance won't you? With
      the Master Builder?

Ragnar
   I can't really –

Solness
   come on a little
   just a little, just for me

He starts to dance towards Kaja.

Kaja
   oh okay –

Solness
   why shouldn't we dance?
   bloody hell we deserved this, all of us
   it's a celebration for all
   it isn't just me
   we are a bloody dream team
   the Master Builder's dream team

*He is dancing in a silly way, making them all laugh.
There is some hilarity, even Ragnar laughs, despite
himself.*

Solness gets out his phone.

   let's take a selfie
   Kaja, you can put it on the website –
   the team that got the Master Builder title

They all stand in a line.

Solness takes the photo.

couldn't do it without any one of you. You know that?
a toast to all of you. If only you'd smile you'd be
bloody marvellous.

Beat.

He dances a bit to himself.

I got Master Builder UK
I got Master Builder UK
I work with three miseries but I got fucking Master
Builder UK

Brovik carries on clearing up the mess.

for goodness sake leave it

Ragnar
I told him

Solness
we all work too hard,
we have to open the new building on Monday
from tomorrow it will be all hands to the pump after
this award
let's drink now
yes?
Tell you what Kaja, get some port from upstairs and
tell my wife to come down here

Kaja goes.

*Brovik mouths to his son to go, and leave him to talk to
Halvard.*

Ragnar (*mouths*)
are you sure?

Brovik nods.

listen I'd love to stay but

Solness
really, you're going?

Ragnar
it's been a long day, and tomorrow

Solness
fine fine, go.

Ragnar
Kaja too, she's as exhausted as me

Solness
me and your old man will sit up a bit, yes

Brovik nods.

Ragnar leaves.

Solness
you know I have this godawful feeling it was me

Brovik
what was you?

Solness
I think I was standing here
no here
just at the moment when the Lord Mayor came in
just before we all went off to that lunch –
I think I was, could I have been

He looks at the bottle.

I think I put the fucking cigarette in the bottle
can you imagine, I did that?

Brovik
can I have a word?

Solness
or maybe I came back after the lunch, before that tea

Brovik

it is just there is so little time to talk during the day

Solness

talk?

Brovik

and as you know my health

Solness

I thought you were better?

Brovik

that's what I told them, Kaja and Ragnar

Solness

you aren't better?

Brovik

it's not clear

Solness

what does that mean?

Beat.

good grief

Brovik

I wish I was joking

Solness

but we celebrated, we thought that was the end of it

Brovik

I know

Solness

we thought you could put it behind you, I can't do
this if you aren't

Brovik

I won't die before the opening

Solness

don't talk like that, don't even –

Beat.

shit

Brovik

this wasn't what I wanted to say

Solness

shit, Brovik

Beat.

Brovik

it was actually Ragnar, I wanted to talk to you about

I mean it's all connected but –

Solness

isn't he happy?

Brovik

it's not that, it's not about happiness

it's become a bit more pressing though, what happens

to him

if I go, if I

Solness

I'll get you to the best doctors

Brovik

you said you'd make him permanent

Solness

wait, stop all this 'if I go' stuff

we won't talk about it until it happens

this Master Builder award the work it will bring

Brovik

exactly

you'll need people around you

good people

Solness

I'll need you, Brovik, I need you –

Brovik

you'll need young blood
you'll need to train up the young

Solness

yes of course, we've talked about this

Brovik

Ragnar is hungry
he and Kaja are about to get married, he needs a leg-up

Solness

and I'll make him permanent, in the end

Brovik

you haven't really given him a chance

Solness

that's not fair, I have given him chances –

Brovik

he's better than you think

Solness

he can be sloppy, you've said yourself

Brovik

yes he is sloppy at the odds and ends you give him
he could be more disciplined, I admit

Solness

it was more than that

Brovik

the crumbs you give him though

Solness

not crumbs, please don't be like this

Brovik

the Lovstrand house, give it to Ragnar

Solness laughs out loud.

Brovik doesn't.

Solness
oh that isn't a joke?

Beat.

give it to Ragnar? Really, do you think?

Brovik
you don't care about it, you said yourself

Solness
is this actually serious, you are asking –?
they aren't just people, they're well-connected people,
    they are –

Brovik
if he could have something he could get his teeth into

Solness
I love Ragnar and I'd love to help him out but –
he isn't qualified technically

Brovik
you could oversee it

Solness
I'll do it myself, there is no problem with the
    Lovstrand house you are talking about it like –

Brovik
you don't have time, you said yourself

Solness
I'll make time
I can't believe we are discussing this, we have the
    opening on Monday –
I know he is your son and of course he has talents

Brovik
you would rush it through quickly rather than give
    my son a chance?

Solness
    they wouldn't like it anyway
    the couple
    he is too young, he hasn't got –

Brovik
    they met with him today

Beat.

Solness
    today?

Brovik
    yes

Solness
    while I was off getting the award, the same 'today'?

Brovik
    they liked his ideas

Solness
    I'm finding this a bit hard to hear

Brovik
    Ragnar just needs a chance

Solness
    he actually met with them, are you being serious?

Brovik
    yes Halvard, he met with them

Solness
    well what did they say?
    come on, you told me he met with, he met with them,
        what did they say?

Brovik
    they were impressed
    they liked his ideas
    they thought he was very innovative, modern

Solness

what and I am traditional? Is that what they meant?

Brovik

don't be like that

Solness

so I am the traditionalist now? Of all ironies

Brovik

would you look at his plans?

Solness

he has done *plans*?
this can't have been the first time he met them

Brovik

he met them a few times, yes

Solness

a few?
what is that? Two, three?

Brovik

I don't know exactly
he has some new ideas, you know because he keeps
    trying to talk to you about them –

Solness

fucking hell, 'modern' ideas?
he met them *four* times?

Brovik

I didn't say *four*

Solness

enough to make plans
enough to convince them he was 'modern'?

Brovik

alright

Solness

this is how you want the day of the award to go, this is how you send me away from the biggest fucking day of my life?

I thought we were friends

Brovik

we are friends

Solness

good friends, best friends

Brovik

we are, but this is my son

Beat.

Solness

you know I don't want to fight you, particularly if you, if this . . .

Beat.

and you are sure he is up to it?

Brovik

yes absolutely

Solness

he had better not fuck it up, if I have to pick up the pieces

Brovik

you won't. I appreciate it. Are you saying yes?

Solness

he is lucky to have you to fight his corner

Brovik

that's a yes?

Solness

yes yes

Brovik
  yes!

Solness
  yes, okay, yes.

Brovik
  I can't wait to tell him

Brovik starts to go.

Solness
  you aren't going to sit up with me, chew the cud?

Brovik
  I just want to break the news

Solness
  well bring them back, we can keep drinking

Brovik
  it's been a long day, everyone is tired

Solness
  of course. Of course

Brovik
  don't be like that

Solness
  not intended. 'Master Builder UK', it's a big thing
    isn't it

Brovik
  it's a brilliant thing. And well deserved

Solness
  remember the day you took me on
  I guess I was like Ragnar then, hoping for a scrap

Brovik
  it was one of the best moves I made

Solness
even when I bought your company out?

Brovik laughs.

Brovik
well, we all have to fear youth. In some ways.
You've done good. I'm proud of you

Solness
we've all done good

Beat.

Brovik
I'll see you in the morning, yes?

Solness
goodnight dear friend

Brovik
look at his drawings, you might be surprised

Brovik walks out.

Solness sits alone for a second.

Pours himself some more wine.

Drinks.

Thinks about it.

Gets up, goes over to the plan chest.

He gets the plans out.

Solness
okay let's see what you've got

He looks at the plans carefully.

The Lovstrand house.

Then he looks at them again.

He knocks some stuff off the table to make space.

He studies them.

the fucking sod

He takes his phone out.

Kaja can you come back here
well make an excuse

He puts his phone down and looks at the plans again.

He puts them down on the table and scrutinises them.

Aline comes in.

Aline
there you are

Solness doesn't answer her, he is still engrossed.

She takes her shoes off and starts to rub her ankles.

Christ
I thought I had met boring people in my time
but bloody hell, that do –
are we going for dinner?

Beat.

I actually came to find you
everyone kept saying congratulations and where is
    your clever husband Mrs Solness?

Beat.

another round of awful conversation
the general gist of which is that no one can wait to
    see the new shopping centre opened on Monday
'we are so lucky to have an architect like Halvard
    Solness'
'and what will it be like this new pantheon?'
well I guess it will have shops in it, I say
and a tower
'ooo a tower'

there is a lot of interest in the tower
'a shopping centre with a tower'
all my husband's work has towers, it's a kind of
    hangover from when he was doing towers. And
    anyway so the conversation goes on –
where is he I thought to myself? The Master Builder
why am I enduring all this if he isn't even here –?
someone has put a cigarette butt in a bottle of wine
look Halvard –
who the hell would do that?
they have actually put a cigarette butt inside a good
    bottle of wine

Beat.

She turns to him.

there'll be even more on Monday

Solness
more what?

Aline
all this, hullabaloo

Solness
I suppose –

Aline
you ready for it?

Solness
contractor says yes all ready to go.
I'll go over tomorrow but –

Aline
if Prince Charles really is now coming in person
the telly no doubt
not a case of whether you want it now
you've got it –

Solness

    I like it

Aline

    you get an award like this, you get everything that
        goes with it

    city is proud anyway, are you actually smiling?

Solness

    I'm actually smiling

Aline

    let's go and eat something?

Solness

    in a minute

Aline

    don't tell me you're working?

Solness

    not really, just a few things –

Aline

    what could be so pressing that –

Solness

    it's youth isn't it?

Aline

    what is?

Solness

    Brovik is right. Everyone says that you should worry
        about getting old, but really it's the young we
        should be scared of

Aline

    I thought you weren't going to get drunk –

Solness

    I've sobered up

Aline

you only get philosophical when you have drunk
too much

Solness

it's not that –

Aline

what is wrong with you then?

Solness

Ragnar

Aline

Ragnar?

Solness

he's quite good it turns out
that's the thing

Aline

what?

Solness

unexpectedly

Aline

you said he was incompetent
months you have been saying he is basically foolish

Solness

not only is he good, he has taken in everything that
been going on around him
he's actually a damn fine architect

He shows her.

plus he's got ambition

Aline

so what's the problem?

Solness
he spoke to – met with the Lovstrand couple, behind
my back

Aline
does Brovik know this?

Solness
he orchestrated it, it seems and
those bloody people, the ones that could never decide
not only made decisions but
let him draw it up for them

Aline looks.

Aline
this is for the Lovstrand house?

Solness
yes

Aline
the difficult Lovstrand house that has taken months?

Solness
yes

She looks again.

Aline
and it's good?

Solness
I'm as surprised as you
it's very good
I wouldn't have put the stairs where he has but –

Beat.

Aline
what is that?

Solness

it's what they fucking asked for
it's the impossible
this halfwitted fanciful idea they had in their heads
that I said couldn't be done more to the point
he did it, he designed a roof that did just what they
said it could do, and with a view

Aline

how?

Solness

because he thought about it
because it appears he is damn clever at this
because he has taken my idea and evolved his own
twist
because he wanted it to work
maybe because he liked them and this wasn't just
another job for him
I don't know how he made it work, look
because he is 'modern', young, because he thinks
differently?

Beat.

it's the fucking impossible
in one roof-shaped drawing

Beat.

Aline

I never really know how to read a plan

He turns it the right way around.

oh

She moves it around.

Solness

but now I wonder if I should get rid of him

Aline

what?

Solness

I don't want someone competing with me, we have
    to be a team
I thought we were a team
but no, he's like I was at his age

Aline

you just got the Master Builder plaque

Solness

yes but two years from now
with ideas like this –

Aline

I don't understand you

Solness

I just got lucky, after the fire
I had land I could build on
no one thought I could do it, a lad like me, no training
I had to be ruthless, play fucky fucky, undercut,
    I bought out his dad's company

Aline

it was all above board

Solness

Ragnar can do it properly. He's got all the advantages,
    I never had

Aline

so?

Solness

so I don't like it

Aline

you've nothing to fear
you're brilliant. You always have been –

Solness

your parents didn't think that

Aline

they would now

Solness

if I had had what Ragnar has

Kaja comes back in.

Kaja

you wanted something?

Solness

I want you to dictate a letter, do you mind?

Kaja

now?

Solness

yes to the Lovstrand couple, now

Aline and Kaja look at each other.

it's still early isn't it, the day isn't over?
it's only just gone seven for God's sake
don't look like that, both of you know I don't switch
    off easily, and with all this wine
did you get the port?

Aline

I thought we were going to go for dinner?
you told me endure the afternoon and we would
    go for dinner

Solness

can we do that another day?

Aline

well there's the opening on Monday

Solness

after the opening, life will calm back down

Aline

I don't know what has happened to you in this last
hour but we can talk over some pasta –

Solness

please remember how it works, when things have
to be done, they have to be done

Beat.

He looks at her.

Aline

so, what, I am supposed to make scrambled eggs for
myself upstairs
and you go back to work?

Solness

I'll make something later

Beat.

Aline

remember the days when every problem we would
puzzle over together?

Solness

its just one evening, don't make it a big thing

Beat.

He has gone back to the plans.

Aline

it's alright Kaja, I brought the port

She throws a bottle at him.

Aline goes out.

Kaja and Solness are alone.

Kaja feels a bit awkward about what has happened.

Kaja
you want a letter typed?

Solness
yes

Kaja
to the Lovstrand couple?

Solness
it won't take long

Kaja
so you are going to let Ragnar do it?

Solness
just dictate the letter.
is that too much to fucking ask Kaja, only I believe
I pay you?

Kaja
no of course

She goes and gets a laptop.

Solness
dear Mr and Mrs Lovstrand

Kaja
I think he is a professor actually

Solness
Professor fucking Lovstrand then

Beat.

Kaja
and she's a doctor

Solness
are you serious?

Kaja

I think so, yes. I can check

Solness

next you'll be telling me their daughter has an OBE?

Kaja

the daughter is just thirteen

Solness

I know about the daughter, I was joking.

of course I know the daughter, spent enough time in
their kitchen being polite

Professor fucking Lovstrand, and Dr fucking
Lovstrand, take this down just as ascribed Kaja
please

Beat.

He tries to think of what to say next.

Kaja looks a bit unnerved.

Solness

I don't want to have to sack Ragnar. I need people
on my side

Kaja

oh God

Solness

and I like him, I always have

plus if I sack him, you'll all have to go

the three of you, you are like three points on a triangle

I couldn't keep one of you

Kaja

you're mucking about, you're drunk

Solness

how do you know?

Kaja

you wouldn't do that to Brovik
Brovik is like your soul

Solness

the good part you mean?

Beat.

Professor fucking Lovstrand. Dr fucking Lovstrand.
This is what I get for all those hours sitting around
your kitchen table, drinking your shit coffee, eating
your inedible cake. Laughing at your terrible jokes,
smiling at your boring daughter, and making out
that your house, your extension, your tiny corner
of the universe is the most interesting, the most
important . . . behind my back you go to one of
my juniors

Beat.

keep typing. I understand my office trainee Ragnar
Brovik has been in to see you. I have to say I was
amazed to learn this since I believed I was handling
your account. I wondered if you could possibly
drop by the office to explain the situation or even
better fucking pick up the phone to the heir to the
throne and tell him that he just gave the Master
Builder plaque to the wrong person

Beat.

Kaja

do you want me to send this?

Beat.

Solness

you should have told me

Beat.

stop typing

She stops.

Beat.

They look at each other.

He comes over to quite near her.

Kaja
    it's quite late, do you want me to type something
        else, only –

Solness
    I'll ring you a taxi, in a minute
    why was it that we stopped talking?

Beat.

    I'm just interested

Kaja
    we –

Solness
    yes?
    remind me
    look at me would you. You always told it to me
        straight whatever it was that was going on

Beat.

She looks at him.

Kaja
    not really

Solness
    outside, last summer
    on the pavement outside, almost every day
    cigarette in our hands, what was going on really in
        the office, when there was that problem in
        accounts, could even say we became friends
    and so I think it's fair to ask why?

why did all that stop?
if it hadn't stopped you might have warned me, you
    might have said Brovik and Ragnar are up to
    something but
was it something I said?

Kaja
no

Solness
so . . .?

Kaja
I got

Solness
what?

Kaja
I suppose, I got
nervous

Solness
nervous?

Kaja
yes

Solness
of what?

Kaja
of your wife

Solness
my wife?

Kaja
I thought she . . .

Beat.

Solness
no go on, say –

Kaja
I thought she thought it was less innocent than it was

Beat.

and as it didn't matter –

Solness
I see
it didn't matter?

Kaja
there is a kind of force-field around her, when she
comes near –

Solness
she thought that it was less innocent than it was?

Kaja
she is your wife, of course she would have an opinion
if you were spending time with me

Solness
but it was innocent as you say –

Kaja
of course it was

Solness
then what had she to fear?

Kaja shrugs.

Kaja
I don't know

Solness
exactly

Kaja
it was just a feeling

Beat.

do you want me to type an actual letter or not?

Solness

I haven't decided yet
and I know it's time for you to go home
and I know you are engaged to Ragnar

Kaja

I am not sure where this is leading –

Solness

I only said that to reassure you
the friendship we had was innocent
you are with Ragnar, I am with my wife
but I miss it. A bit

Beat.

and then you gave up fucking smoking so I was
    outside on my own
lah lah, e-cig bollocks
leave a man standing out the back

He gets out a packet of cigarettes.

He starts to light one.

tell me again why you gave up?
oh yes Ragnar doesn't like it

Beat.

not *you* don't like it, *Ragnar* doesn't like it
he doesn't like it because he could see you were
    standing outside smoking with me
and he could see you from the office
they control you
the pair of them
my wife controls me, they control you
the three of you working in the same place
I'm just saying
what am I saying?
have a fucking cigarette

He passes her a cigarette.

if you want to
no control coming from me
your choice of course

She takes it.

He lights it. She inhales.

She looks grateful.

Solness
it's almost worth giving up smoking to have that first
pull of an illegal fag isn't it?

She laughs a bit.

tell me I am fucking right

Kaja
alright you are fucking right

Solness
will you tell me what they are planning?

Kaja
I don't think there are plans
I don't think it is like that

Solness
Ragnar must realise he could set up his own firm
      in time
and with the contacts from here –

Kaja
he wouldn't take them

Solness
so he does want that?

Kaja
I am just saying he's moral, he wouldn't do it

Solness

is he moral though? That's the question
he seems rampant
and most of his ideas are ones that have come from me
maybe he won't while Brovik is alive maybe, but
    Brovik tells me he won't last forever
what is to stop Ragnar moving on once his dad has
    gone?
I looked at the other things he has done
it's not just the Lovstrand house

Kaja

Brovik just wants you to make him a partner
I think if you do that –

Solness

that's the only chink left to me

Kaja

what do you mean?

Solness

at the moment he is newly qualified, and under me
I thought he was crap – no problem but now I know
    he is good
and the minute he gets anything built, anything of
    scale

Kaja

but you will sign off. You have to, if he is as brilliant
    as you say –

Solness

and then he is my arch rival standing in front of me
it's bad enough he stops you from smoking but

Beat.

I know I know, I'm being ridiculous but
why in my right mind would I make him a partner?
    Or now anyway?

I'm only asking the question. It's interesting isn't it?
Here is the challenge, promote the person who is
destined to overtake you

She holds his gaze for a moment

They stand quite close.

Kaja
I can't believe you even think like that

Solness
you can't?

Kaja
you're ruthless

Solness
not ruthless but I worked my way up the hard way
how else do you get to be Master Builder?

She smokes the cigarette.

Kaja
and this is revenge –

Solness
this, no?
how could this be revenge?

Kaja
having a cigarette with his fiancée?

Solness
not at all

Kaja
presumably you want me to do something –

Solness
possibly, not sure

Kaja
I won't

Solness

I think you might
I don't think you liked being told to give up smoking
I don't think you like being watched either

Beat.

persuade him away from the Lovstrand house
give me another year or so
let me get my head together about Ragnar
you can tell him I thought the plans were dreadful
    if you like or
a man needs a woman to look at him and tell him he
    is great
if she doesn't then – it erodes him

Kaja

why would I do that?

Beat.

Solness

okay
maybe you wouldn't
barking up the wrong tree, I shouldn't have asked

Kaja

you think my loyalty is to you?

Solness

call it a hunch

Kaja

you're a bit of a bastard

Solness

you liked standing outside on the pavement with me
you liked that I chose to share a cigarette with you

Kaja

you're full of shit actually

Solness
    really?

She puts her cigarette out.

Kaja
    yes, really really full of shit

Solness
    okay

Kaja
    I don't like you
    you've got it all wrong
    you bought the cigarettes, I was bumming off you

Solness
    I see

Kaja
    yes we were smoking together but only because I
        could joke about it later

Solness
    fine

Kaja
    and my loyalty will always be to Ragnar, you dick
    I love him.

Solness
    I get it

Kaja
    do you? Or did you just try to manipulate me?

Solness
    okay, I'm sorry I misjudged

Kaja
    you used to say the team thing was the most important

Solness

Ragnar blew that didn't he?

Kaja

what? By being good?

She starts to walk out.

Solness

Fuck it Kaja, I made a mistake. I need you, we have
got the opening on Monday

Kaja

you need all of us. But it's your name on the building.
You prick

She leaves Solness in front of the plans.

Solness

damn it, damn it all

*He looks at them. He fiddles with a corner. He makes a
tiny tear.*

*Just a little at first, then he takes the whole thing and
scrunches it up.*

He roars as he does it.

A man walks in.

Dr Herdal

I know exactly how you feel.
there's a young student asking for an autograph by
the way

Solness

send them away

Dr Herdal

and me? Should I send myself away?

Solness

I'm in a godawful mood Hans

Dr Herdal
good, so am I
watching my best friend getting a medal has put me
in a real downer.
let's go to a club –

Solness
piss off

Dr Herdal
you won't sleep tonight anyway

Solness
I might, if you give me something

Dr Herdal
no chance, might as well go out on a bender

Solness
I've got to stay sober until Monday

Dr Herdal
oh come on, couple of nightcaps

Solness
can't you prescribe something?

Dr Herdal
I've given you everything. Who wants to sleep anyway?

Solness
I do. Sometimes. Sometimes I want to calm down and –

Dr Herdal
how's the blood pressure?

Solness
fine

Dr Herdal
still taking the tablets?

Beat.

Solness
don't turn me into an old man

Dr Herdal
you're turning yourself into an old man

Solness
plenty men have high blood pressure at my age

Dr Herdal
and diabetes? And glaucoma? And a cholesterol
reading that is through the roof –

Solness
just because you have got no one to go home to

Dr Herdal
guilty as charged
but if you would prefer to go up to Aline and I'll
go back to my empty flat

Solness
she's making scrambled eggs

Dr Herdal
she certainly knows how to live

He takes something out of his pockets.

I've got these, don't know what they are really but
the pharmacist say they keep you up

Solness
let me see

Dr Herdal
prescribed for heart attacks

Solness
fucking hell

Dr Herdal
moderated release, last all night
come on, you look miserable they won't harm you

Solness
even with blood pressure and diabetes?

Dr Herdal
especially

Solness
I can't keep up with you
I wish you would just get yourself another wife

Dr Herdal
why would I want one of those?
is there anything you actually need to do for Monday?

Solness
not much, odds and ends

Dr Herdal
I think if we break the capsule we could snort it
no, don't think the empty flat is a problem, the empty
    flat is bliss
and it doesn't have to mean it is always empty
oh yes

They break the capsule and Dr Herdal snorts it.

come on
where is your get up and go?
and don't say get up and gone

Solness laughs.

that's the spirit, get this inside you
then let's hit the town
two hours we'll be back, Halvard and Hans like old
    times

Solness snorts it.

He waits to feel the effects.

Solness
nothing yet

Dr Herdal
no?
disappointing
oh hang on
the practice nurse said
oh yes

Solness
mild

Dr Herdal
yes mild but kind of twinkly

Solness
I suppose

Dr Herdal
oh reaching all the extremities now. That is where
    it needs to go. There is actually a cigarette butt in
    a perfectly good bottle of wine here
who the hell would do that?
so go on then, what the hell is wrong with you? On
    your special night?
look at all these cards, these well-wishers –

Solness
I know

Dr Herdal
it's all over the news, picture of you and the mayor
prince turning up on Monday
students wanting autographs
got to hand it to you
don't tell me the new building is a turkey

Solness
no, it's not that

Dr Herdal
then what?

Solness

I don't know, something about being at the top?

Dr Herdal

I've never been at the top of anything, I wouldn't
know

Solness

I have got the fucking Master Builder plaque for
God's sake

Dr Herdal

what's going on?

Solness

I was standing there, this afternoon when I got the
plaque thinking
here I am
this is actually happening
and then the next moment, a sort of depression

Dr Herdal

you'll stay at the top for a little while surely

Solness

but really, the only way is down – what other option
is there
our time of lives, you already said I am crumbling

Dr Herdal

you need to take care of yourself, that is all I said

Solness

okay, so imagine when you are finally senior partner
you'll do that for a bit then
some other fucker will come up and bite you

Dr Herdal

it doesn't work like that

Solness

well you're lucky

with me, I'm only as good as my last job

yes I got the plaque, Prince Charles will come and cut
the ribbon – but I got it for work I was doing years
ago. All those ideas I put into this building, I
dreamt up years ago. What do I actually do now?
Where are the new ideas? And the fucking royalty,
I mean I am glad he is coming don't get me wrong,
but – Charles – he's an old codger, a traditionalist

Dr Herdal

take another of these

Solness

plus I am making mistakes

forgetting things

yes

people usually catch them for me

I have always made mistakes but I used to be more
careful

I really nearly fucking blew

last month a miscalculation that would have cost us,
Monday's opening might not have happened

and who picked it up, the least qualified person in
the office

Ragnar

I hate it

age

and then I get resentful

Dr Herdal laughs.

Dr Herdal

you don't know age

when you work in my profession you really see age

Solness

okay, not age

decline

it might be shallow at the moment, but I'm on a slope

Dr Herdal
we're all on a slope. Let's go to a club, pick someone
up

Solness
I get dizzy sometimes

Dr Herdal
maybe lose a bit of weight, take some exercise

Solness
feel like I might stumble –

Dr Herdal
come and shag someone senseless, you'll feel better
don't tell me you don't do that any more?

Solness
I promised Aline

Dr Herdal
you always promise Aline, so?

Solness
I'm trying to change

Dr Herdal
who was the girl that just left?

Solness
Kaja, my PA

Dr Herdal
looks nice

Solness
she is
but not for me
I have been a fucking awful husband, that's another
thing
Aline knows it, I know it. She watches me, she
watches me around the women in the office and

fair dos. I should be better. I should give her what
she wants. That woman has put up with years and
years of shit
shit that you and I got up to together

Dr Herdal
you can't be regretting –

Solness
I'm just saying, your wife walked out on you, but
mine stayed. Maybe in this era of decline, she finally
gets what she wanted
you have to strive to be happily married don't you?
You have to work. No corners. You have to work
the hard way, work the long way

Dr Herdal
you're right, you're in a funny mood

Solness
I always had this luck
this incredible good fortune
I wanted something, I got it
I wanted a woman, I only had to say, I want you to
myself
but that Kaja, that woman just now
something has changed
I just got the fucking plaque and she normally flirts
with me
I know how it is with her, or how it was
She –

Dr Herdal
we all get to this point

Solness
not me

Dr Herdal
everyone loves you

you'll wake up tomorrow with a hangover but
    everyone loves you

Solness
    not the young
    the young hate me
    they're just waiting, mistake by mistake
    seriously I think that
    we'll pull him down they are saying
    you wait
    you wait Master Builder UK, you wait!
    you're fading, there's nothing new in your work now –
    your brain doesn't work like it used to
    make room, make room!

Dr Herdal
    you should have had children, there's nothing to fear
        from the young, they are all fucked up and on their
        phones all day

Solness
    you're wrong, they are all malign
    fuck it, I should rip it all I . . . I should throw them out

Dr Herdal
    who are you talking about?

Solness
    the young
    the hideous grasping youth.
    and yet I won't. I'll roll over and give it to them. As
        always, for what else can I do?

There is a knock at the door.

Dr Herdal starts to go towards it.

    leave it
    I'm in no mood

Dr Herdal
    it's that student that I told you about

Solness
then definitely leave it

Dr Herdal goes over to the door.

Dr Herdal
I had a long chat with her, she's doing a dissertation

Solness
please don't

Dr Herdal
she's a bit of a fan, just a few questions about some
church somewhere

Solness
my head aches

Dr Herdal
it'll do you good
have someone remind you of your achievements –

Solness
I can't remember them

Dr Herdal
shall I really tell her to come back another day?

Solness
which church?

Dr Herdal
the one at Lysanger

Solness goes over to look out of the window.

does that look like the terrible grasping youth?

He goes to the door.

I mean watch out, she might rip your head off with
her architecture dissertation
Beat you to death with those bosoms of hers.

Solness
very funny

Dr Herdal is laughing.

Dr Herdal
tell you what, you talk to her, I'll go and eat some
of Aline's scrambled eggs, then we'll all go out.
Aline as well. We have to keep celebrating. Only
thing that staves off decline. Inebriation

A young woman, Hilde Wangel, walks in.

Hilde
is there some joke?

Solness
sorry no
we were just –

Hilde
only he said I might be able to ask you a few questions

Dr Herdal
I'll leave you to it
better put your armour on

He leaves, laughing to himself.

*Hilde comes right into the office. She isn't sure of the
joke.*

Solness shrugs, like he isn't sure either.

She takes a chair and moves it to quite near Halvard.

He is a bit unnerved.

He moves his chair a bit further away.

She moves hers nearer again.

Solness
so . . . you had some questions for a dissertation?

Hilde

don't you recognise me?

Solness

my friend said you were a student, am I supposed to –

Hilde

I am, I was of course but
da dah

Beat.

Solness

have we met before?

Hilde

sorry?

Solness

only I think

Hilde

yes we met before
are you joking?

Solness

what was your name?

Hilde

very funny

Solness

only I think, maybe you've got muddled?

Hilde

hang on
da dah
maybe my hair was shorter
da dah
and I might have been a bit shorter too
da dah
I had braces actually
da dah

Beat.

He's totally at sea.

    my name is Hilde
    Hilde Wangel

Solness
    and I know you?

Hilde
    you came to build the church at Lysanger

Solness
    ah – Wangel
    okay, I know your father
    a dentist isn't he?

Hilde
    a surgeon

Solness
    oh
    yes okay, a surgeon

Hilde
    anyway its not about my father, here I am –!

Beat.

    I didn't know you could be so cruel, if this is a joke –

Solness
    listen, I am very happy to go through some questions,
      if you are actually a student?

Hilde
    you don't know why I am here at all do you?

Solness
    not a clue

She laughs a little at that.

    you're making me nervous now

Hilde

the Master Builder, nervous?

Beat.

is there any more wine?

Solness

were you at the party?

Hilde

yes I came down this morning.

Solness

you were invited?

Hilde

no but if you just have the right attitude and say you
    are, then people let you in
you have to sort of hold your head up and look like
    you know where you are going, I admit but I am
    quite good at that and so no one asked
I realise it would have been easier if I wasn't wearing
    jeans but
I don't like dresses
I don't much like jeans either
I don't really like clothes at all in fact, much better
    to stand in nothing don't you think?

Beat.

Solness

why did you want to go to that party?

Hilde

to see you of course
to see you get the plaque

Solness

I think you're a spy
I think this is some game
send a beautiful girl to turn my head, distract me

68

Hilde

I'm not a girl, I'm twenty-five

Solness

I think someone has sent you from one of the other
firms

Hilde

to what end?

Solness

to knock me off course, or to get secrets

Hilde

how exciting, secrets!

He realises she is being ironic, is teasing.

Solness

what then?

Hilde

do you really think that, a spy?

He looks at her.

Solness

are you actually a student?

Hilde

I am yes

Solness

of architecture?

Hilde

what else is there to study?

Solness

and you are writing a dissertation?

Hilde

of sorts

Solness

you have some questions?

Hilde

I have lots of questions
but we can get to them later

Solness

later?

Hilde

in the morning, when you haven't drunk so much

Solness

now wait a minute, the morning?

Hilde

your wife remembers my family better than you have
she said I could stay for a night

Solness

are you kidding?

Hilde

my mother and she were friends
the wife of a surgeon and the wife of an architect had
    lots to discuss

Solness

she said you could stay here?

Hilde

she took pity on me I suppose
I spent everything I had on the train fare down
I don't have any cash for a hotel and as you can see,
    I have no suitcase
no nothing in fact

Solness

are you actually insane?

Hilde

very likely
are you?

He laughs.

Solness

okay fair point. Am I actually insane?
very possibly

Beat.

Hilde

they should have given you the plaque years ago
after that church in fact, before that even

Solness

you think?

Hilde

yes I think
all those fools that got it instead. The years of
uninspiring work that got lauded, and there you
were being passed over

Solness

not quite

Hilde

the way you build spires, there are actually books
written about it

Solness

not many

Hilde

you're being modest
you create the impossible in one spire-shaped piece
it's like you defy gravity

Solness

no wait a minute

Hilde

we actually had to write an essay on them
    second year
when you started you redefined gravity
we had three lectures on that spire alone
a whole lecture series on your work
I wanted to tell everyone I know him, he came to
    my house once and he and I

Solness

what?

Hilde

he is friends with my father
I wanted to tell them all that

Beat.

there is a half-written email here

Solness

I don't think you should look at that

Hilde

dear Professor fucking Lovstrand and Doctor fucking

Solness

that's my secretary

Hilde

is she deranged?

Solness

we were mucking around

Hilde

hilarious

Solness

she'll delete in the morning
come away

Hilde

you need a good secretary

Solness

she is a good secretary

Hilde

haven't you got the shopping centre opening on
Monday?

Solness

it's not a shopping centre, it's a –

Hilde

whole new way of living, of course. I understand that
the point is you have an opening on Monday and she
has time to muck around?

Solness

not really, none of us do

Hilde

is she married?

Solness

who?

Hilde

this secretary

Solness

really is this any business of yours –?

Hilde

she isn't then

Solness

engaged, but so what?

Hilde

you'll lose her, she'll go off and have babies

Solness

    maybe I will
    but not before Monday

Hilde

    imagine this is an interview, for a student paper
    I might actually write it
    who is the Master Builder, the man behind the glory?
    the man behind the revolution in modern living

Solness

    alright, but ask about me not my secretary

Hilde

    do you like the people you work with?

Solness

    sometimes

Hilde

    is she pretty?

Solness

    enough!

Hilde

    maybe you need young blood, maybe you need
      someone who won't put the word 'fucking' when
      they address a client

Solness

    ah, so you are asking for a job?

Hilde

    not sure yet
    probably

He laughs again.

    oh you are thawing out. Very good.
    alright, second question, how do you come up with
      your ideas?

Solness

is this an actual question?

Hilde

this is an actual question

Solness

for an actual dissertation?

Hilde

for an actual dissertation

Solness

you start with a brief
you speak with the client
you think a bit

Hilde

you think a bit?

Solness

alright you think a lot

Hilde

I read somewhere that you take inspiration from
nature
you said God used to be reflected in your designs

Solness

did I say that?
that must have been some years ago

Hilde

so you don't think that now?

Solness

well there is always a reflection of the natural
form but

Hilde

you don't believe in God?

Solness

I struggle

doesn't everyone?

Hilde

hang on, I need to write this down. Do you remember
Lysanger

Solness

of course. Lysanger was the biggest, the most ambitious
it was an important stage for me doing churches
I liked the endeavour, seeing a community. I wanted
to give them something that would reflect . . .
I don't know
yes I suppose God was in it somewhere

Hilde

can I quote that?

Solness

what is your actual dissertation on? On Lysanger in
particular or –

Hilde

it's on you

Solness

okay

Hilde

that's it really
just you

He laughs, despite himself.

what?

Solness

I find you curious.

Hilde

oh
okay, I'll settle for curious just now

She takes a bottle moves to drinks from it.

is this okay, if I have a drink?

Solness

I'm not sure. Aren't you a bit young to knock it back?

Hilde

I'm twenty-five I told you
ughh God it's got a cigarette in it

She spits it out.

He laughs, passes her another.

Solness

alright, but if you are staying with me and my wife
don't drink so much you puke as you go upstairs

Hilde

I never puke

She drinks.

this one is better.
want some?

She hands it to him.

Solness

I think I've had enough

Hilde

so have I but I never know when to stop when I am
nervous

He takes it, drinks.

Solness

why are you nervous?

Hilde

of you

Solness

of me?

Hilde

that you would've forgotten everything.

Beat.

Solness

I'm not sure I understand what you mean

Hilde

then I was right to be nervous
I knew I should have drunk more

Solness

okay so we met but –

Hilde

it was the day the tower was being got ready

Solness

yes I remember the day, the opening of course
always a big moment for me, and Lysanger of course

Hilde

it's not the day, I'm talking about, it's the evening
what happened later –

Solness

you know I wonder if we should go upstairs, my
wife is cooking scrambled eggs and she would
remember more than me

Hilde

she won't remember this part

Solness

since then I have put up lots of towers on lots of
churches –

Hilde

none as big as that

Solness

I agree

Hilde

it was the first time you were able to realise your
ambitione

Solness

yes in a way

Hilde

you climbed up carrying the big wreath to the top

Solness

I always used to do that, I only stopped because
I started to get dizzy
I suppose it was showing off

Hilde

it was raining. Slippy. Some were saying it was too
dangerous for you to go all the way up, but the
whole town had put on this celebration and to not
have the wreath put up felt like it would disappoint

Solness

I remember that

Hilde

music in the churchyard, local and amateur I guess
but. Hundreds and hundreds of people. And the
whole school – I was there, dressed in white. With
flags

Solness

oh yes the flags were brilliant

Hilde

we had a flag specially designed for the town

Solness

yes, they wanted me to put a flag up there with the
wreath

Hilde

you should have done

Solness

I thought it would kind of –

Hilde

wreck the design?

Solness

yes I suppose I did

I do remember taking the wreath up there, and you
   are right it was rainy. I had to climb the scaffolding
   and the wood was slippy, they said I should use a
   wire, clip myself to the frame but I didn't want to.
   I guess I was arrogant in those days –

and those flags, the whole school waving flags

Hilde

I was one of them

down there with my flag, going crazy in fact

we had done a project on the new church spire and

and then watching this man, this actual alive man
   climb to the top

Solness

it was fucking high

Hilde

you didn't look dizzy

Solness

well, looks can deceive

Hilde

you weren't though were you?

you looked like man approaching God

and then you sang

Solness

no

Hilde

yes we all heard

Solness

I don't sing

Hilde

when you got to the top you let out this kind of song

Solness

I am sorry to say, I think you're exaggerating –

Hilde

it sounded like harps in the air

He laughs.

Solness

okay

I really can't sing but okay

harps in the air –!

tell that to my wife, she won't let me sing in the
    shower

Hilde

anyway it's not that part that is important

it's later that the real thing happened

Solness

the real thing?

Hilde

the reason I am here

Solness

I thought you were here because you are writing a
    dissertation

Hilde

I'm here because we made a promise

Solness

we did?

Hilde

you must remember the evening. There was a dinner
for you in the club

Solness

vaguely yes

Hilde

you knew my father of course already

Solness

the dentist

Hilde

the surgeon, he was your host

Solness

okay, if you say so

Hilde

you were invited back to our house, after the dinner

Solness

listen, if you were a child I can see that these details
might have meant more to you

Hilde

it's not just detail
it's what happened between us when we were alone

Solness

we were alone?

Hilde

you weren't so dismissive of me then

Solness

how long ago was this?

Hilde

you said that I looked beautiful in my white dress
you said I looked like –

Solness
listen, Miss –

Hilde
call me Hilde

Solness
I don't know where this is going –

Hilde
you said that when I was big you would come for me,
I just had to wait

Solness
was I drunk?

Hilde
you'd been drinking yes
I could taste it on your tongue

Solness
on my tongue?

Hilde
you held me in your arms, you bent me backwards
and you kissed me

Beat.

Solness
you must be mistaken

Hilde
why would I be mistaken?

Solness
misremembered then

Hilde
don't say you will deny –

Solness

of course I will deny it, that church spire was what five – seven years ago?

Hilde

ten

Solness

so you were –?

Hilde

I was fifteen

Beat.

Solness

you can't have been fifteen

Hilde

I was

Solness

then I don't remember a thing

Hilde

it was the summer I turned sixteen, but I was still fifteen

Solness

well you can't have looked fifteen, did I know you were fifteen?

Hilde

I don't know

Solness

I bet you were wearing make-up or something, maybe you told me you were eighteen

Hilde

you do remember then?

Solness

of course I don't

I don't actually remember a fucking thing
you could be making the whole thing up
you *are* making the whole thing up

Beat.

fifteen
good grief

Hilde
what's the problem?

Solness
do you understand what you are saying?
this is an accusation

Hilde
you kissed me

Solness
so, what, you are going to make a complaint?

Hilde
no

Solness
listen I don't know what your game is –

Hilde
you said you would come and get me, all I had to
do was wait ten years and then
so I waited ten years

Beat.

He looks at her.

we are the same you and me

Solness
I don't think so

Hilde
you said I was too young to run away with then,
but now –

Solness

look I have not always acted like the best
I haven't been a good husband but I am not a bloody –
God, do you realise what you are accusing me of?

Hilde

I didn't come to make an accusation
you aren't listening –

Solness

but you realise you have
I must have been fucking drunk
oh bloody hell

Hilde

I didn't mean –

Solness

what happened after the kiss?

Hilde

more kissing

Solness

okay what happened after more kissing?

Hilde

you put your hand down my front
you kind of cupped

Solness

so you did have breasts?

Hilde

of course I did

Solness

and after?

Hilde

you sort of were holding me, like this, you started
reaching for my skirt

Solness

    Jesus Christ

    and then?

Hilde

    do you mean did we do it?

Solness

    yes that is of course what I am asking. How far
        did it go?

    Jesus what do you think I would be asking?

Hilde

    no we didn't

    we didn't do 'it'. We didn't do anything other than
        kiss really

Beat.

Solness

    thank fuck

    thank Christ

    we didn't, you are sure?

Hilde

    yes

Solness

    thank the Lord

Hilde

    but not because we didn't want to

    because we were disturbed

Beat.

Solness

    we were disturbed?

Hilde

    we were

Solness
by who?

Hilde
my father

Solness
the dentist –

Hilde
the surgeon

Solness
sorry surgeon, surgeon

Beat.

He looks at her.

She looks at him.

Hilde
he didn't see but
he never let your name be mentioned in the house
   again

Solness
does he know you are here now?

Hilde
it doesn't matter to me, all that stuff

Solness
Christ alive

Hilde
I came back later
I found you later

Solness
don't tell me there was a later –?

Hilde
later was when you told me you would come for me.
like a troll you said. All I had to do was wait ten
  years and then you would steal me away

Solness
I'm sorry about that

Hilde
don't be sorry, I wanted it

Solness
what can I say? I'm sorry about everything
I was drunk
I had drunk too much
I must have thought you were older
thank God we did nothing

Hilde
we didn't do nothing

Solness
okay I kissed you, Jesus don't hang me for a kiss

Hilde
I love you, that's all

Beat.

Solness
what?

Hilde
I love you. And I have waited

Solness
listen, I don't know what you are expecting but –

Hilde
I know it won't be easy

Solness
easy?

Hilde

I know you have a wife and of course you are busy,
   you have the Master Builder title now and have this
   opening on Monday but
your secretary, the one that is about to go off and
   have babies

Solness

she isn't about to have babies

Hilde

I could do her job. You have women running about
   for you. Use me
I'm not fifteen now, its not illegal
I just want –

Solness

what?

Beat.

Hilde

you started something with me
you kind of pushed a button in my body
I hadn't felt anything like it
and when we didn't –
it's like I have missed it

Solness

listen

Hilde

and if there is any chance –

Solness

Miss –

Hilde

I don't care where
I don't care how

Beat.

once would do but more if you are willing

Solness
I think you should go to bed

Hilde
exactly

Solness
please, Miss Wangel

Hilde
tell me that you don't remember anything of that
night

Solness
it's starting to come back

Hilde
I was wearing a white dress

Solness
that isn't what's coming back

Hilde
you don't need to flinch. Don't worry, I haven't come
to take anything from you. I haven't come to
destroy all this. I just want to be part of it. To be
near you

Solness
will I get that in writing?

Hilde
you need it in writing?

Solness
no sorry, I just
I think I am a bit in shock
I know I can be a wanker but –

Hilde

you said you would build a kingdom for me
there has to be a place, however small, for the two
of us
that's what I want

Pause.

Solness

you don't know me
you have this idea in your head, this is a humdinger
of a crush in your mind, but the reality
you see all this and you think

Hilde

I know you better than you think

Solness

great man, awards, openings

Hilde

I don't care about that stuff

Solness

it's become an obsession

Hilde

yes a bit, but so what?

Solness

you're actually scaring me

Hilde

I'm not crazy
I'm just want you

Beat.

I want you. In all ways
you can do what you want with me. You can have
me. I won't get between you and your wife but . . .

Beat.

Solness is a bit taken aback by the boldness of this offer.
He takes a sip of water, tries to think straight.

Solness

one thing I don't understand

okay, I see what you are saying and clearly I behaved
like a jerk or a drunk bastard, and gave you all this
hope but

ten years, that's a long time

why didn't you even write to me?

Hilde

you told me I shouldn't

Solness

and that was enough?

Hilde

you said all I had to do was think about you, and
you would know it

I knew that wasn't true of course but I did think
about you

whenever there was an article about a new building
that went up, a picture of you in the paper

you are remarkable

by my pillow, I kept a file, under the mattress

no one knows your achievements better than me

when you challenged the government on their policy,
when you built the civic centre, when you went to
London, advised the Lords

Solness

you kept it all?

Hilde

I have been your biggest fan

Solness

you are really –
a little crazy perhaps, but

Hilde

don't send me away

Solness

what you want, you realise –

Hilde

I know
I know
mad eh?
yes crazy
but why really? I am a woman now, you are a man
I think we would be good for each other

Beat.

Solness doesn't know how to reply.

plus I want to be an architect myself one day
you need a work experience

Solness

my wife is fragile, I can't just

Hilde

we won't hurt her
I just want to adore you, help you. Make you even
greater if I can. The future is yours Halvard Solness,
no one knows better than me what you can still
achieve

Solness

I'm at the end of my career in a way

Hilde

bullshit, you are just at the start. You can't think
like that, you've got the best ahead

Dr Herdal comes back in.

Dr Herdal
scrambled eggs are ready, your wife insists you come
and eat something. Surely enough discussion of
architecture for one night?

Solness
okay – will do

Dr Herdal
Hilde, are you going to join us?

Hilde
may I?

Solness
er . . . yes

She picks up her cardigan and goes.

Dr Herdal looks at the Master Builder.

Dr Herdal
so your encounter with youth? Did she eat you?

Solness is still trying to work out what just went on.

what is it, what did she want?

Solness
nothing

Dr Herdal
you don't look any the worse for it anyway

Solness
really?

Dr Herdal
absolutely
if anything you looked a bit flushed –

Interval.

Act Two

The next morning.

The Master Builder is alone in the office.

He is cleaning up.

He manages to make a space to work.

He gets his laptop out and starts to work.

He can't actually think.

He wipes his eyes, tries to wake up. Tries again.

He gets a large glass of water and puts two dissolvable paracetamol into it.

He stirs it around. Knocks it back.

No good.

He goes to the cafetière, knocks back some cold coffee.

No good either.

He goes to his drawer, takes out a cigarette.

Is just about to light up when Aline comes in.

He sees her.

Solness
I was just having a little –

He puts the cigarette away.

fucking stonker of a headache

Aline
me too
you working?

Solness
    kind of.

Aline
    much to do?

Solness
    as always, last minute details
    snag with the plumbing, what a surprise

Aline
    you need to change firm

Solness
    too late, anyway they'll sort it
    and then there is this problem with getting the
        scaffolding down in time, I told them we cannot
        open a modern icon, with royalty and the TV, if it is
        covered in scaffolding. And the fire alarm sprinklers
        need to be plumbed in, that's not actually the
        plumbers' fault but
    I thought you were asleep, I tried to creep out

Aline
    did either of us sleep?

Beat.

    what are you going to do about Ragnar?

Solness
    put it off. Get to the opening, then tell him to stick in
        his fucking place

Aline
    is that what she told you to do?

Solness
    what?

Aline
    the new work experience, our house guest

Solness

don't be absurd

Aline

well you seemed to spend most of the evening talking
to her

Solness

blame Dr Herdal, he brought her in
and she told me you'd agreed to let her stay

Aline

she told me that you'd said that

Solness

okay, so we'll tip her out

Aline

did you see how much she drank?
She practically sat on your lap after dinner

Solness

we'll give her the fare to go back to her parents

Aline

do you want that?

Solness

of course I want that
why wouldn't I want that?
she's a loose cannon. I've got the opening tomorrow
she can go home

Beat.

she didn't really sit on my lap, did she?

Aline

she was flirting

Solness

mucking around

Aline

you were flirting back

Solness

I got the bloody plaque yesterday, I was jolly. Listen
I have got so many things on my mind –

Beat.

He looks at her.

She looks at him.

what?

Aline

nothing

Solness

is there any chance you could see that something
really good just happened here?
I got the Master Builder plaque for 2017. Architect
of the year
that we are in the middle of three rather extraordinary
days
Prince Charles is turning up to open my new building
tomorrow
everything that I have been working towards and
doing for us
yes for me but for us,
could you just for once say, maybe you could say well
done.
and yes maybe I was mucking about a bit because
maybe for once, I was feeling a bit carefree and like
life was okay
is that so bad?

Aline

well done

Solness

don't stress yourself

Aline

you know I'm proud of you

Solness

you don't look it

Beat.

Aline

I am actually proud
of all this, of course
yes I am proud but

Solness

. . . what?

Pause.

Aline thinks.

Aline

it wasn't always like this, was it?

Solness

please Aline

Aline

this fog we live in

Solness

there is no fog

Aline

you know what I mean

Solness

I need to get on to this problem with the sprinklers,
I'll need to go down there

Aline

okay

Solness

sorry, can we talk later?

Aline
  so, what, should I make her breakfast?

Solness
  if you like
  or don't, doesn't matter
  tell her to buy a croissant on the way to the station

Aline
  how long is she supposed to be staying?

Solness
  I didn't say exactly how long, I just said okay
  I can say, on reflection –

Aline
  can you do that, can you take it back?

Solness
  on reflection I don't have the capacity for a work
      placement right now, sorry
  and that will be the end of it

Beat.

Aline
  we go to marriage counselling, they say infidelity is
      a symptom not a cause. You have to listen to what
      it is saying

Solness
  for fuck's sake

Aline
  what?

Solness
  there is no infidelity

Aline
  don't even –

Solness

alright, but there is no infidelity with *her*

Aline

well not yet –

Solness

don't be ridiculous, she is what –?

Aline

twenty-five

Solness

I am fifty-seven, yes of course I have looked, flirted, you know

Aline

she sat on your lap

Solness

she didn't, she *nearly* did. We were all drunk. I was off my head, thrown by the Ragnar thing, Brovik being ill

Hans gave me these tablets, I don't know what they were, maybe it was that

blame him

Aline

sometimes I think, why am I not enough?

Solness

Aline

Aline

sometimes I actually have that thought, then other times I think of course I know. I know really, I know where we went wrong

Solness

we didn't go wrong

Aline

if I had kept that baby, if I had given you a child

Solness
Jesus, Aline

Aline
you needed a son

Solness
of course it's not that

Aline
what is it really that I am?
a joke?

Solness
you have to stop this

Aline
I'm a shrivelled-up old thing and who wants that?

Solness
listen to me, you can't think like this
anyone should be so lucky to be with you

Aline
but –

Solness
I'm flawed
we both know it, I'm a terrible human in some ways
I'm a wanker, I think with my prick
I've never hidden that from you, I try you know I try
I'm not good, I'm greedy, I want what I can't have
I don't know, I was made wrong
I have always been flawed, you knew I was flawed
    before we got married.

Aline
people say to me they all grow up in the end, just
    wait, he'll change
someday he will turn around and thank you
and from then on

Solness

there is nothing wrong with you, you have to believe
that

Aline

so why can't you love me?

Solness

actually I do
that is the absurd thing, I love you very much

Aline

tchhh

Solness

you know I love you very much. If not you should

Beat.

Aline

I don't want to come to the opening on Monday

Solness

you're taking this right out of proportion. I haven't
even touched her

Aline

it's too much, the plaque, the opening

Solness

I'll get rid of her

Aline

you should never have invited her in

Solness

you have to be there on Monday
I want you there

Aline

I feel too old to start again

Solness

we've been through this before, I thought we –

maybe you should have married a different man
your parents always said

Aline
don't start that

Solness
well leave me then, why don't you?

Aline
as simple as that?

Solness
you obviously want to, I get fed up of all this, I am
not up to you, nip nip

Aline
you get fed up?

Solness
yes I get fed up. Just look at what I can give you.
Please for once

Aline
maybe we *are* done then

Solness
oh for fuck's sake

Aline
every attempt by me to fix something, and you get
angry

Solness
enough! Just enough. I am in the biggest three days
of my life. If you can't see that then that's your
problem. I'll get rid of the girl, it was a stupid
mistake, okay? But I am not all bad

Hilde walks in.

Hilde
good morning

your single bed – your spare room
I felt I could have slept for a million years

They both stare at her.

what?
have I said something wrong?

Aline

not at all

Hilde

what do you want me to start with?

Solness looks at his wife.

Neither of them answers.

you said I could be useful –
is there a problem?

Solness

it's just there's a lot going on and on reflection, the
timing

Hilde

don't send me home

Solness

I don't want to send you home but you have to
understand, taking on a work experience, it means
a commitment and with this opening tomorrow –

Hilde

no please

Aline

oh for God's sake, Halvard, let her stay.

Hilde looks from one to the other.

I can't bear the pleading. The doe-full eyes

Solness

are you sure?

Aline
 is it up to me? Really? I say she can stay and she can
  stay?

Solness
 no of course not, of course
 this is my decision and I say –

Aline
 I can't be bothered with this any more
 you should know what to do, you shouldn't need
  to be told
 if you want her to stay and she wants to stay, have
  a fucking picnic

Aline walks out.

Hilde is left with the Master Builder.

His look follows the way that Aline had gone.

Hilde
 I didn't mean to stir up trouble

Solness
 it isn't that

Beat.

Hilde
 should I just go then, should I go home?

Solness
 yes
 you should

Beat.

Hilde
 she said it was okay?

Solness
 I know she did, but she didn't mean it

Beat.

Hilde
do you want me to go?

Solness
yes

Hilde
actually to go?

Beat.

Solness
yes please

Beat.

Hilde
all because of her, because she doesn't like me?

Solness
no, it's me she doesn't like

Hilde
should I just go upstairs and get my stuff?

Solness
yes, exactly

Hilde
walk to the train?

Solness
yep

Beat.

yep you should

Hilde
that word again, 'should'

Solness
okay go

Beat.

go

Hilde

I'm going

Beat.

I have to say though, I'm good at typing, I can file
things, I can sort out your technology, make an app
I got an A in computing at A-level, I can blow up
balloons I can pour wine, put up ribbons
I can be really helpful, you've got the opening

Solness

I think you should go

Beat.

Hilde

you really mean it, you are telling me to go?

Solness

I just did

Hilde

tell me again

Beat.

It's getting harder for Solness.

They are standing quite close now.

He's torn.

Solness

go

Kaja walks in.

She clocks the two of them.

Kaja

I left a message, did you –? Did you get my message?

Solness

I heard the plumbing is not finished, the sprinkler
system isn't working yet, I was just going to go
down there

Kaja

Brovik's in intensive care

Solness

what?

Kaja

we had to call an ambulance in the night

Solness

you serious?

Kaja

he had some sort of seizure

Solness

fucking hell, is he okay?

Kaja

Ragnar wanted me to come in and tell you in person
no he's not okay
he's not woken up

Solness

oh Jesus, but hang on, yesterday he was –

Kaja

it doesn't look good, I'm warning you

Solness

so what do we do?

Kaja

I brought all this from home
in the ambulance, I was thinking about what you
would need for tomorrow, without him

Solness

we'll manage, won't we? You and me

Kaja

you'll manage, not we
none of us will be here

Solness

none of you?

Kaja

we'll be by his bedside

Solness

but –

Kaja

he is my father-in-law. I don't have a dad
and I'll have to be there for Ragnar
he's dying, Halvard. Today, tomorrow
the doctors don't think he'll wake up at all

Solness

fucking hell

Beat.

fucking hell. I understand I understand but
I can't just stop the opening –

Beat.

Kaja

the catering needs to be signed off. These ones here
and that should be paid in advance, I have made a list

Solness

okay

Kaja

and this is the list of dignitaries for tomorrow

Solness

alright

Kaja

the police have the list as well, they need everyone off
site at eight a.m. sniffer dogs, the whole lot. The
Prince himself won't get here until ten to three.
That is a change from yesterday. Ten minutes
earlier, he wants a tour from you before the actual
opening. Press photos on the steps. That is not clear
when, needs checking. Three of the photographers,
some need access arrangements, I can be on the
phone of course but

Solness

yes

Kaja

and these are the list of press that have contacted us.
They all want interviews today, I was going to get
back to them this morning, I guess you'll have to
do that now –

Solness

thank you

Solness has taken everything that he has been handed.

He looks rather lost.

Kaja

will you manage?

Solness

I'll have to. Would you . . . kiss his forehead for me –
I'll run over to the hospital the minute I can

Beat.

please know that when it comes to that man –

Kaja

I know

Kaja goes.

Hilde and Solness are left.

Solness
fucking hell

Hilde
I can sort out the list of dignitaries

Beat.

I can sort out the access
liaise with the press

Solness
I need to get on site, there are all these last-minute
snags

Hilde
I can do the catering. Take over the cheque

Solness
I guess these labels just need typing up

Hilde
I can do that too

Solness
please don't nip at my head

Hilde
I won't

Solness
anything else is –
I have to get through this opening
it's the biggest opening of my life, and without my
colleagues
well this is serious, years I have been working on
this building

Hilde
I understand

Solness

this site, it's a whole new –

Beat.

Hilde

I can get all that done by lunchtime
and more, you tell me what to do

The Master Builder looks at her.

Solness

have you ever liaised with press before?

Hilde

I can do anything

Beat.

don't you ever think, some things are meant to be?
That things happen for a reason –
or more than that, that there might be . . . some sort
of . . . beings out there in the universe looking out
for you

Solness

looking out?

Hilde

you said that to me

Solness

I said that?

Hilde

at Lysanger
that you sometimes thought you had helpers
I am the same. I believe there are ways in which I am
helped. I get what I want. Always. However bad
it is, however much I know I shouldn't want it,
I just have to ask, I just have to say God or hell
or some angel, I want that

and it comes
this is my fault. I wanted to stay, you were about to
    send me away then I asked the universe and wham
    this man Brovik is ill

Solness
it had nothing to do with you

Hilde
so you don't know what I am talking about?

Beat.

I sometimes wonder if there is any limit to what
    I could ask for

Solness
you are a strange girl, you know that

Hilde
together we could be something remarkable

Solness
I have to get through the opening

Hilde
but after, you and I
I am as terrible as you

Solness
I'm not terrible

Hilde
you want things that are out of reach, and so do I
you want things you shouldn't even think

Beat.

Solness
alright I sometimes think I have a troll within me

Hilde
that is it exactly, a troll

Solness

it's a kind of ruthlessness isn't it though, that's all?
Wanting to better yourself

Hilde

it's a sort of illness sometimes

Solness

exactly
you do have it too

Hilde

sometimes it frightens you

Solness

I am often frightened
yes that's true

Beat.

They look at each other.

Hilde

together we can be whatever we want to be
we're soulmates

Solness

you think that?

Hilde

what else is it?

Solness

there is such an age gap, you are still so young

Hilde

we are the same, who else has what we have?

Solness

I caused a fire. Not with my hands but with my mind.
That was the worst. My parents-in-law, they had all
this land but they wouldn't let me build on it, and

I wanted, I wanted that land and I knew that if the
house caught on fire

Hilde
then one night –

Solness
yes

Hilde
had you asked for it

Solness
of course I had

Hilde
out loud

Solness
yes

Hilde
so, the trolls

Solness
only I had to pay. It meant I could start my career
and of course I built the new house straight off but,
I paid dear

Hilde
you were guilty

Solness
no I wanted that house to burn, no it was my wife
she was pregnant, and that night
getting her out of the house, she nearly died, and the
baby, a little boy

Hilde
I see

Beat.

Solness

there is always something to pay. The trolls help you, but you have to give something to them. Something precious

Hilde

you aren't giving them me

Solness

no I'm not giving them you

Ragnar comes in.

Ragnar

where's Kaja?

Solness

she was just in

Ragnar

I've come for my drawings, Dad said you would hand on the commission

Solness

I will look at them, I said I would

Ragnar

so you haven't looked yet

Solness

I haven't

Ragnar

or you have, and you didn't like what you saw

Solness

no, not that

Ragnar

Dad wants to know it is all settled. They think he will die today or tomorrow

Solness
okay

Ragnar
that's it, 'okay'?

Solness
I said I would look –

Ragnar
alright. Alright Master Builder, Mr Big Shot
I was trying to save you from it

Solness
save me from what?

Ragnar
you've already lost that contract

Solness
what?

Ragnar
the Lovstrand couple don't want you anywhere near
their house

Ragnar notices Hilde for the first time.

who's this?

Solness
work experience – Hilde, meet Ragnar

Ragnar
you never stop do you

Solness
I don't know what this is or

Ragnar
they won't have you through the door again, the
Lovstrand couple

Solness
I know you're upset, and understandably

Ragnar
they say you flirt with their daughter

Solness
what?

Ragnar
they say you and she, that you aren't safe around her

Solness
now wait a minute

Ragnar
you want to know why Brovik sent me, to calm it
down

Solness
it's ridiculous

Ragnar
I don't know what happened, but yes, they don't
want you in their house

Solness
I never even met their daughter

Ragnar
not what they are saying –

Solness
well are they making a complaint? This is absurd

Ragnar
I don't know yet

Solness
I don't understand what is going on here, are you
making some kind of threat?

Ragnar
no threat from me

Solness

I never even smiled at their daughter, I mean I met her,
    maybe I was friendly but –

Ragnar

we were all trying to save you from this
we thought if I did their house, we could hush it up,
    whatever happened, a misunderstanding or –

Solness

Brovik knew this?

Ragnar

I could try to appease them, we could do a cut-rate job

Solness

so this is blackmail?

Ragnar

it's too late
it wasn't blackmail, it was rescue
you arsehole can't you see that? It was fucking rescue
you should have just let me do the house Halvard
you know I am up to it

Solness

I didn't even smile at her

Ragnar

you understand what the stakes are, you lowlife?
doesn't matter what you did – that is what you are
    being accused of.

Solness just stares at Ragnar.

where are they anyway, the drawings?

Ragnar sees the drawings and gets them.

He has to de-scrunch them.

Solness

there is not a scrap of evidence

Ragnar

you've started to sink

Solness

I could fight this if I wanted, it's absurd

Ragnar

go ahead

Solness

utterly absurd, pernicious

Ragnar

call it what you want

Solness

and damaging, we have the fucking opening on
    Monday, the press. Everything that couple are
    saying is lies

they hated me from the start, and wanted or – oh yes,
    you and Brovik came up with a way to get the
    house. You got it right out from under me, one
    sniff of something like this

Ragnar

are you going to let me do it or not?

Solness

tell me that's true, you put the idea in their heads
you are the one that's devious here

Ragnar

just say it. 'The Lovstrand house is yours, Ragnar'

Solness

the bloody envious schemer in my own –

Ragnar

can you say that? Those few words?

Solness

do you really hate me so much, you would see me
    lose everything to get this house?

Ragnar
believe what you want

Solness
believe? Yes that's the word, who in their right mind
would believe

Ragnar
just say the words

Beat.

just say the words, just say the words, what's the big
deal, just say the words

Solness
have the fucking house

Ragnar
at last

Solness
get out of here, I don't want to see you again

Ragnar starts to walks out.

Ragnar
I'm on to you, Solness, you know I am.

Ragnar has gone.

Solness
cretin, snake in the grass
this isn't the end of the story. This whole thing is balls
it's okay Hilde

He and Hilde stand in silence for a second.

Beat.

when you get to be in a position like mine
it's nothing, it's really fucking nothing. Why is he
doing this?

Beat.

Hilde

I believe you

Solness

good, so you fucking should. There is nothing there. nothing whatsoever. Oh Jesus, I can't believe this I'm a good man. I have always been a good man

Hilde

I know that. No one knows that more than me.

Act Three

Dr Herdal and Halvard.

Solness
I didn't by the way

Dr Herdal
Jesus

Solness
in case you are wondering, I didn't –

Dr Herdal
how old?

Solness
I don't know

Dr Herdal
you must know –

Solness
fourteen I think. Or thereabouts –

Dr Herdal
bloody hell

Beat.

are the police involved?

Solness
no
no of course not, no

Dr Herdal
hell Halvard

Solness

I think I can deal with it, I just needed to get out the
house

the point is I didn't fucking touch her, that is the point

so you would think if there was any justice

Dr Herdal

you didn't touch her?

Solness

of course I didn't, don't be absurd

Dr Herdal

well, what do they want?

Solness

who?

Dr Herdal

the couple, the parents

Solness

they want Ragnar to do their house

Dr Herdal

easy, yes?

Solness

yes, they went a cut rate

Dr Herdal

so give it to them

Solness

I have

that isn't the issue

they can have what they fucking want

it's Ragnar

it's what he wants

Dr Herdal

and what's that?

Solness
his dad, Brovik is dying –

Dr Herdal
Brovik, I thought he –

Solness
Ragnar fucking wants part share in the company

Dr Herdal
he what?

Solness
that's what he wants
part share

Dr Herdal
he's distressed, he's worried –

Solness
just because I gave him the house, he thinks he can ask
for more

Dr Herdal
or what?

Solness
exactly, or what?

Beat.

Dr Herdal has to think for a second.

Dr Herdal
you can do him for blackmail

Solness
you think anyone will listen to me? Blackmail or not –

Dr Herdal
yes but –

Solness

Ragnar has got a bit of dynamite in his hand, and he
    is ready to throw it
doesn't matter if I touched that girl or not, the truth,
    what the fuck is that?
all he has to do is breathe it
he knows that, one little breath and

Dr Herdal

he really, he would do that?

Solness

he hates me, he'd do that
I missed a trick with him, I should have brought him
    on before
he is good, I didn't see it. I didn't want to see it
and of course we are all upset about Brovik's illness
but this –

Dr Herdal

you should go to the police

Solness

how can I do that?
don't be a fucking wanker
who the fuck is going to believe me?
and anyway, I have the fucking Prince of Wales
    turning up to the opening
the damage will be done

Beat.

I bet he planned it like this

Dr Herdal

can you make him partner?

Solness

tcch

Dr Herdal

can you though?

Solness
in theory
but what else would he want?

Dr Herdal
have you got any choice?

Solness
I don't know, have I got any choice? You tell me
you're the clever one

Beat.

Dr Herdal
what actually happened with this girl?

Beat.

Solness
nothing

Beat.

really nothing

Dr Herdal
no bullshit

Solness
no bullshit, fuck all

Dr Herdal
Halvard

Solness
seriously, nothing

Beat.

Solness
she touched my knee, Hans
I was the one that moved her hand off. That's all
I was sitting around her parents' table, we were all

there, her mum and dad, and I feel this little hand
on my leg. Well it was hot in that room and I – she
rubbed her hand up my leg a bit

Beat.

I moved it off. Course I did.
and outside later, I told her. I didn't like that, I said
she's a sulky cow. Trying it on
her parents think she is a child, but she is no child
she wanted to see if she could get some kind of
    reaction from me
she's at that age where she wants to see what her
    power is – you know. They are all the same at
    that age

Dr Herdal
are they?

Solness
fourteen is the worst, tits all ready
want to see if they can move a man
see how far it can go
why else would she put a hand on my knee?

Dr Herdal
they aren't all like that

Solness
I'm not talking about your daughter, if that's what
    you're thinking, your daughter is fine, different
this girl, Lilian didn't want anything, she just wanted
    to see if it would have an effect.

Dr Herdal
and did it?

Solness
it made me angry, yes
and I told her, later, outside

you shouldn't do that I said, there are men –
I want men she said
I don't like it. Don't do that again I told her

Beat.

Dr Herdal
and that was it?

Solness
and that was it
or I thought it was
yep
absolutely the end of the story

Dr Herdal
then you're okay

Solness
you think I'm okay?

Dr Herdal
did anyone see you talking to her?

Solness
course not

Dr Herdal
did anyone see her putting her hand on your knee?

Solness
she's pissed off I knocked her back
and this is revenge
she's one of those, plays games

Beat.

maybe I shouldn't have told her like I did, but what
else was I to do?

Dr Herdal
and Hilde?

Beat.

Hilde?

Solness
what about her?

Dr Herdal
what happened with her?

Solness
Hilde is different

Dr Herdal
why is Hilde different?

Solness
if you can't see it –

Dr Herdal
you tell me

Solness
I thought she was fucking eighteen. That's why it
is different
I kissed her, yes

Solness
ten years ago I kissed a sixteen-year-old and now I am
going to be put in a cage, really?

Dr Herdal
wasn't she fifteen?

Solness
whose side are you on?

Beat.

Solness
okay, yes fifteen, sixteen, a month off being sixteen.
not much difference

Dr Herdal
you've done stupid things

Solness
I know I have
I kissed someone I thought was older, okay
I don't deserve to lose everything, or you tell me – do I?

Beat.

Dr Herdal
alright
no you don't
you're an idiot, a fool
you play close to the wind you always have
but okay

Dr Herdal breathes out.

Solness
you know I am not one of those –

Dr Herdal
I know
I do know actually

Solness
right

Dr Herdal
but we need Hilde out of the way, she can't be part
   of this

Solness
I thought she was older honestly, and it was a fucking
   kiss

Dr Herdal
I get it now

Solness
you weren't sure –

Dr Herdal
I had to think, yes sure, but

Solness
we're okay?

Dr Herdal tries to think.

Dr Herdal
when is the opening?

Solness
three-thirty

Dr Herdal
and Ragnar?

Solness
he wants an answer by noon

Dr Herdal
I guess you're going to have to give him what he
wants

Solness
my worst bloody nightmare

Dr Herdal
is there any halfway house, any –

Solness
I don't know
I don't even want to speak to him

Dr Herdal
you have to get through today, whatever it takes today
give him what he wants, say yes you'll do it

Solness
and then?

Dr Herdal
then tomorrow is different

you don't have the Prince of Wales breathing down
    your neck tomorrow
you can go and see the parents of this girl tomorrow
you can smooth it over
tell them what you told me, if she did this to you,
    likely she has tried it on with someone else
you might be surprised
they could be reasonable

Solness
will you come with me?

Dr Herdal
Aline is the person you need
you need Aline at your side
she and you should go

Solness
we're not in a good place

Dr Herdal
well get in a good place

Beat.

that's the first thing
get in a good place with your wife

Solness
I could get properly screwed couldn't I?

Dr Herdal
that's not going to happen

Solness
alright.

Beat.

They look at each other.

Dr Herdal
alright

SCENE TWO

Aline

I lay out my dress. And shoes, get them ready. Fix the buckle. Not every day that I get to meet royalty

stand in my bra and pants, see a bloody ladder in my tights

should have thought to get new tights. What is wrong with me? Why can't I even sort out my tights? I thought about every other bit but missed that

Halvard comes in, face looks different. He looks puffy, jangled

where have you been?

no answer

not an unreasonable question is it – 'Where have you been?'

comes over, stands in front of me. Gives me a kiss unasked

what was that for?

Solness

do I need a reason?

Aline

no just –

kisses me again

Solness

you're a beautiful woman that's all

Aline

what?

Solness

you're my best friend you know that, Aline

Aline

what the hell is going on?

Solness

nothing, can't I say that?

Aline

course you can but –
we've got to get going, Halvard

Solness

fine. Later then
I'm glad to have you here by my side, that's all

Aline

you've hardly spoken to me for days

Solness

I'm talking now aren't I?

Aline

and he is I suppose he is talking now
I take his hand, squeeze it. I hope it goes well for you
today, love
he smiles. I don't know what this is about, but I think
I like it

Solness

thanks
let's hope it goes well for both of us

Aline

my mobile is ringing. Can't find it, fuck it – can never
find it. Can hear it faintly
you okay, got everything you need?

Solness

yes yes, perfect

Aline

go downstairs, mobile is in my handbag
number I don't know
hello? I say, yes?
a woman's voice

is that Mrs Solness?
yes, I say again
it's Mrs Lovstrand here
heard about her, difficult according to Halvard, what
     the hell does she want? Haven't got much time
     right now
only I would really like to talk to you, she says
Halvard at the top of the stairs, hang on a second
     I say to the phone

Solness

can't find my tie

Aline

on the dresser

Solness

who's on the phone?

Aline

Mrs Lovstrand

Solness

who?

Aline

Mrs Lovstrand. He is coming down the stairs now,
     two at a time

Solness

put it down

Aline

what?
she says she wants to talk, excuse me a minute

Solness

put it down

Aline

what the hell?

comes and grabs the bloody telephone out of my hand
and when I go to try to get it back

Solness
I slap her

Aline holds her face.

Beat.

Aline
he slaps me
phone on the floor. Smashed I think

Beat.

Solness
I'm sorry

Aline
what the bloody −? Jesus
and tears are coming into my eyes, all these tears

Solness
I don't want you to talk to her

Aline
and that is it? You slap me because you don't want
me to take a call?

Solness
they're stirring up shit

Aline
what sort of shit?

Solness
shit to do with the business, don't ring her back
and if she rings you −

Aline
are you going to tell me what sort of shit?

Beat.

he says nothing but it looks serious, and I can see him
    thinking, debating, should I actually tell her what
    is going on. He looks serious, scared actually, like
    a small boy –

Beat.

Halvard?

Beat.

Solness
we don't have enough time right now

Aline
how long would we need?

Solness
I shouldn't have slapped you
I'm sorry

Aline
don't back away

Solness
I'll get some ice

Aline
tell me what is going on

Solness
I've never done that before, have I?

Beat.

Aline
that doesn't make it okay
my face still stings

Beat.

I go to get the ice. I feel like I have walked over a
    boundary, I'm in some alternative universe now
what the hell is going on and why won't he tell me?

I take the ice back up to the bedroom. My face is red
he's standing in front of the mirror doing up his tie
God knows what is going through his head, I certainly
    can't read it
we'll talk later yes –?
no answer again
Halvard, whatever it is, we'll talk later yes?
after the opening yes?
I look at him, he looks at me
he doesn't even answer

Beat.

    I get out my foundation and I cover up the mark on
    my cheek.

SCENE THREE

Hilde speaks to the audience.

Hilde
    my mum calls me. I'm on the way back from the
    caterers, and I'm in the street, and I have to get to
    the printers to pick up the name badges and I can't
    let him down so I don't answer it. Shove it in my
    pocket. But she calls me straight back, and again.
    And it occurs to me it could be something to do
    with my brother, he might have been in an accident
    or something so I stop in an alcove and I pick it up.
    Mum?
    you have to come home –
    bus goes past I can hardly hear her. What's happened?
    we know where you are, your father is on his way
        down to collect you
    what do you mean?
    you can't be with that man
    he has a name, Mum

what are you thinking? Halvard Solness
he's got Master Builder, and given me a job
have you forgotten? That night, when you were a kid
I was sixteen –
fifteen –
it was a misunderstanding
he assaulted you
I kissed him. I kissed him first –
you were a child
I step into a shop. She needs to be able to hear this.
I kissed *him* though, Mum – and when he pulled away,
    I went back and kissed him again, that is what you
    and Dad never saw. He didn't grab me like you
    think. I spent all day working out how I was going
    to get close to him, and when I got the chance
Mum takes a breath your dad will be at the station
    in thirty minutes
I'm not coming home
if you aren't there Hilde
what? I don't have to do what you say any more.
    I'm twenty-five
I put the phone back in my pocket
she doesn't know him like I do. That's the thing,
    she has no idea who he is
phone rings again, think it's Mum but it's not, its him
the Master Builder.
hello

Solness

    hello
    you been to the caterers?

Hilde

    yes, all done

Solness

    taken the cheque?

Hilde

sorted

Solness

what about the printers?

Hilde

on my way

Solness

okay

you'll bring the badges straight down?

Hilde

yes

Beat.

I will

Beat.

waiting for him to say it
waiting for him to say it
say something or –
maybe not I love you, doesn't have to be I love you
     but I'm looking forward to seeing you, or . . . hi
     you, or . . . I know I shouldn't hope for it but

Beat.

something

Beat.

Solness

Aline thinks it best if you go home

Hilde

what?

Solness

once you have delivered the stuff
go to the printers first, then get on a train

Hilde
what about the opening?

Solness
I've got my hands full Hilde
it was a mistake for me to take you on right now

Hilde
I thought you loved me

Beat.

Solness
I never said that

Hilde
you know how I feel –

Solness
listen, we can't do this today
I shouldn't have said yes to the work experience

Hilde
you said you wanted it, yesterday you thought like
    a troll

Solness
we'll talk later

Hilde
we need to talk now
we are the same you and me

Solness
please deliver the list of dignitaries then get out of
    my hair, Hilde

Beat.

I'm sorry, that was too –

Beat.

Hilde?

Hilde
I can hear him breathing
neither of us say anything
I waited ten years for you

Solness
I know you did

Hilde
another pause
I can feel he is about to put the phone down
Mr Solness I say

Solness
yes

Hilde
hang the wreath today

Solness
what?

Hilde
hang the wreath like you did at Lysanger

Solness
I can't

Hilde
it's not much to ask
could you do that for me?

Solness
I get dizzy, I'm not good with –

Hilde
you are the Master Builder
you can do anything. You forget how strong you are.
    How brilliant

Beat.

I'll be standing at the bottom
watching

Solness
I wish I had your belief

Hilde
together we would have been amazing

Solness
it's changed now

Hilde
you said you would do something for me. Something
    miraculous
let it be that.

Solness
and that will be it?

Hilde
yes that will be it

Beat.

and I put the phone down.

SCENE FOUR

Ragnar
chaos at the site. Sniffer dogs and police.
I text him again. I'm in the Starbucks next to the
    main entrance
where are you?
then I see him
still wearing the same sheen of sweat he was on Friday

Solness
Ragnar

Ragnar

I pull a chair out for the old man

Solness

I'm not staying

Ragnar

you thought about it then?

Solness

you're a cock you know that

Ragnar

does it matter?

Solness

does actually

Ragnar

and you –?

Beat.

Solness

I ought to have fucking taken your daylights out
    yesterday, or years ago when you were just this
    sniffling little squirt that your dad brought in

Ragnar

he's dead

Solness

what?

Ragnar

he died early this morning

Solness

Christ, you say it just like –

Ragnar

thought you would want to know

Solness

of course of course. This isn't funny, this whole cool
  act

Ragnar

I didn't say it was

Solness

you should be at home then, with Kaja

Ragnar

I have the papers. Taken me all day to get the lawyers

Solness

you are really going to do this?
your dad just died – Ragnar, I'm actually quite
  worried about you. If Brovik is dead then –

Ragnar

do you want the opening this afternoon or not?

Solness

can you stop thinking like this for a minute, please

Ragnar

why? one little call to the journalist and a tip-off
  to the palace and I think Charlie will give it a miss,
  don't you?

Solness

you really don't give a shit about anyone but you
  do you?

Ragnar

I learnt from the master.

Solness

this has got to be the end though
no more
you can take your dad's share, alright

Ragnar

I get my dad's share anyway you arsehole.

148

I inherit that
I want *my* bit

Beat.

Solness
then you'll have more than me

Ragnar
it never should have been yours anyway

Solness
you understand I did nothing, that this is all –

Ragnar
I don't actually care
all I care about is being able to work
to do my thing
alright, we'll split the business fifty–fifty, or forty-five–
    fifty-five you can have more
I'm good, I know I am
I just want the chance to be someone

A bell starts to ring.

Solness
that's the drill

Ragnar
I know it's the drill

Solness
we have to get on, that means the royal entourage is
    on their way

Ragnar
I know what it means.
that is another thing, stop speaking to me as if I am
    your junior

Solness
there is so much to sort out, I have to get going

Ragnar

go on then
I am not stopping you, Master Builder

Solness

you couldn't even get the press here if you wanted

Ragnar

see that man over there
a friend of mine
works for the *Evening Times*

Solness looks.

Solness

bullshit

Ragnar

want to speak to him?

Solness

I don't even recognise you any more

Ragnar

that's so odd, because I feel more and more like you

Ragnar hands Halvard his phone.

call your lawyer
I've put the number in
just call him. Tell him to make it watertight

Solness

you fucking arsehole

Ragnar

I'd like to say it's mutual

Halvard takes the phone.

Solness

where have you gone, Ragnar?

Ragnar

same place as you.

Kaja

no one tells you that death is noisy, that there is this
way of breathing, unlike any normal living, that is
to say healthy alive, no this sounds like an animal
like a machine that is off its tracking, that rasps
and rasps and then . . .
the nurse wants to know where his son has gone.
I don't know I tell her. I am not family, well sort
of but
I go outside, stand on the balcony.
I can see the new building from here
they got the scaffolding off
the sun is shining, it looks fucking great. Just what
we all were working towards
the nurse comes and stands beside me
you see that, I say. I worked on that. Or at least
I work for the firm that built that
oh wow she says. Yes I say
supposed to be amazing
it's got towers I say, a shopping centre with towers
five years of our lives more or less
five years and the old man there who just died, he
didn't even get to see it opened
in fact, you see all those police, that is because the
Prince of Wales is coming, today
something bleeps on her I have to go, she says. Tell
your fiancé to come and speak to me about
arrangements
I don't know where he is
I don't know where he is at all any more
in his head or
he isn't with me
it's like he has got some sort of new creature in him,
some sort of animal and I don't like it.

Dr Herdal

and on the spur, I don't know why, I take a second
and I call my daughter. She is with her mum and
we don't speak much but

she answers straight away

hi Dad

hi I say, and I

I don't know I just come out and say it

I have something to ask you love

okay

something, and I want you to answer me, it doesn't
matter and I really wish we were doing this face to
face but

something I need to ask you

you're scaring me

no, no need to be scared, is your mother there

she's in the garden

okay

you know my friend Halvard?

Solness

yes Halvard Solness

the architect?

yes, him

yes I know him

why did you never want him to come to my house?

there's a pause

its really important love, you used to like him when
you were tiny and then after a while

he's boring

I don't think that's it

a pause again, a fucking pause. Why can't she talk
to me?

and I feel this little muscle in my eyelid start to flicker

did something ever happen, love?

another silence. Keep going, I have to keep going now
    I have started
did he ever say or do something that made you feel –
I don't know what to say Dad
please sweetheart, it's important
and I can hear her mother coming into the room,
    what is it she is saying
I've got to go Dad
tell me love
her mother takes the phone
why are you stirring all that up?
what happened? I can actually feel my blood rising
you don't know?
if no one told me –
he's a creep, I told you that. I told you that enough
    times
how old was she?
Twelve says my ex. She was twelve, and he put his
    hand inside her skirt

Beat.

the phone goes dead
I put the phone back in my pocket
I find Aline
she looks at me
and I look at her

Aline

I didn't know

Dr Herdal

you must have had some –

Aline

I didn't know anything for certain
we both had doubts didn't we?

Dr Herdal

don't say I had doubts

Aline
then what?

Dr Herdal
I'm going to fucking kill him
that's what

Aline
what do you want? Me to plead with you – I'd kill
him myself if I had the energy

Dr Herdal
I am going to rip him shred to shred

Aline
I don't even know who he is

Dr Herdal
I go over, I find Ragnar
right, I say. What needs to be done. Let's fucking blow
this up

Ragnar
I got the papers signed, I don't need it now

Dr Herdal
you little prick, it's not just about you

Ragnar
but I can't, I made a deal with him

Dr Herdal
and that's it? Real people got hurt because of him,
real girls
and I push Ragnar away, I punch him and I take my
phone
and I text him. The Master Builder, my old friend.
I know what you did, I text. I know what you did
and I will see you burn

Aline

the mayor's private secretary pulls me over. Where
is he? she says, voice hushed. He is checking the
ribbon, I think. The last few things.
I need to speak to him
how can word have got to her so quickly, that is all
I can think. I need to speak to him Mrs Solness.
I need to speak to the Master Builder

Ragnar

Halvard always wanted a crowd. As big as possible.
everyone come see him, the great I am Mr fucking
fantastic

Aline

she looks at me like something she might have
trodden in. You can't protect him from this. You
know what they are saying don't you? It's lies
I hear myself say

Ragnar

a crowd Halvard, a fucking crowd and they have all
come for you.

Aline

the Prince is coming
the Prince is not coming she says. The *Evening News*
are just about to break the story, a fourteen-year-old

Kaja

I walk out of the hospital, you can see the building
from across the street. There's the buzz we wanted
but – something is up

Hilde

just hang the wreath for me Master Builder, that is all
I want

Ragnar

come over, see the fucker roasted

Kaja

what?

Ragnar

it's all coming for him, the girls

Kaja

I look back at Ragnar, we don't even know

Ragnar

we do

Kaja

why did you choose today? Don't you care about
the building

Ragnar

not as much as you do

Kaja

your father then, he cared. You could have done it
tomorrow, or a month from now

Ragnar

because he fucking deserves it. It's not just about me
and him. Its bigger. And he deserves it this way.
Come over and watch

Hilde

I don't know why this journalist wants to talk to me,
I try to run away from him but he still keeps
following. You don't know him like I do, I shout.
I don't want to talk to you. Go away. All you will
tell me is lies and I don't want to hear. He's going
to hang the wreath for me. That's what he'll do,
and then you'll see. With us it was something, it
meant something

Aline

Mrs Solness, we are looking for your husband.
Policeman now. Kind face.

I look about. Well I don't know, he was here, I feel
    the world start to spin
only we are trying to find him.
I look again. I have to hold on to the policeman I feel
we do need to talk to him. Just a word
I'll find him, he is somewhere in the building
no you are not going anywhere. Sit down
he's got an opening. We know about the opening.
    We'll find him Mrs Solness, don't worry about that

Kaja
    I can see someone starting to climb the building. This
        isn't how it was supposed to be, it was supposed to
        be the Prince and a photo on the front step. Who
        is that?

Hilde
    and it's him, it's the Master Builder

Aline
    and I look up

Dr Herdal
    there the fuck he is

Aline
    he never liked heights, he was never good with heights

Ragnar
    what the fuck is he doing up there?

Aline
    he was a baby when it came to anything –

Dr Herdal
    police have spotted him

Hilde
    he's got a wreath in his hand
    and I see him as he starts to climb even further. He
        is going to do it, he is going to put the wreath right

at the top. He looks down at me. Believe in me, he
seems to say. Keep believing

Ragnar
and there he is above it all

Aline
look at him. Like a bull

Hilde
a clever man, like a genius

Kaja
he has got the fucking wreath in his hand

Hilde
like a matador

Ragnar
what's he going to do, hang it himself?

Dr Herdal
and you have got to hand it to him, he's going to open
the building
arrogant shite

Hilde
even my dad can admire that. When he sees it on TV
the police can see him too. Hear the walkie-talkies,
search is off. We've found him.

Aline
we have to get him down, I tell the police. He doesn't
do heights, journalist in my face. You the wife?

Dr Herdal
and then there is this moment

Kaja
he is dizzy, I can see that

Hilde
he is holding on to the scaffolding

Ragnar
 he has hung his fucking wreath, the bastard got to –

Kaja
 he got that moment after all –

Aline
 then it starts

Kaja
 and I can hear it from downstairs, and I know what
  Ragnar went off to do

Dr Herdal
 a chanting

Hilde
 just a few people standing at the bottom

Kaja
 but they're noisy

Dr Herdal
 Master Builder, kiddy fiddler

Hilde
 few more join in

Kaja
 it takes a while for the words to fix, everyone together
 Master Builder, kiddy fiddler

Aline
 who are they, where have they come from?

Ragnar
 kill the fucker

Aline
 everyone seems to know it
 it's like the whole town knows it

Hilde
 this isn't justice, this is –

Dr Herdal
kill the fucker

Ragnar
kiddy fiddler

Dr Herdal
Master Builder, kiddy fiddler

Hilde
and then smoke

Kaja
can't tell where the smoke starts

Hilde
it comes from the first floor

Kaja
someone has set fire to something

Ragnar
can he hear it above there, up on the tower?
kill the fucker

Aline
smoke visible now, even from where I am standing

Ragnar
kill the fucker

Dr Herdal
police calling for fire engines. Crowd being pulled
back but they are going in

Hilde
chaos, and people running

Kaja
someone is going to get hurt

Dr Herdal
it's like I don't know him, I never saw that man before

Aline
I think yes that is the man

Ragnar
it almost makes you feel –

Kaja
like you don't want to watch

Ragnar
I want to watch

Aline
and then he looks at me. I know he finds me and
he looks at me, and with a look in his eye

Ragnar
what's he doing?

Hilde
we're all there

Aline
he climbs over the safety net

Kaja
he is going over the bar

Hilde
why is he doing that?

Ragnar
police start, sort of panic. Ambulance

Dr Herdal
don't be stupid, we are going to kill you anyway

Hilde
he is on the other side of the bar

Kaja
it's too quick, I can't see, what next?

Dr Herdal
fucking idiot, it was only

Aline
oh God, he's going to jump

Hilde
he's going to jump

Aline
he is actually going to jump –

Halvard comes on stage. The stage changes. Halvard is standing at the top of the scaffolding. Everyone stops.

Solness
what else can I do? you think this is going to be fair?

Aline
come down

Solness
you've got this all wrong

Aline
you need to come down

Solness
none of you can understad me, how can you understand me? Who is going to ask what happened from my point of view?

Ragnar comes out with an official file and starts to read from it.

Ragnar
I was thirteen when I met Master Builder

Solness
none of you are prepared to listen

Ragnar
my mum was a friend of his and we were sitting in a park. I remember I was wearing my school dress

162

Solness
she was no schoolgirl

Ragnar
it was a hot day and I had left school early

Solness
that isn't how it happened

Ragnar
everyone knew Solness, he was kind of famous and he had a face that was twinkly so when he asked did I want to go for an ice cream

Solness
being nice to kids is that a crime now?

Kaja also picks up a file and starts to read.

Kaja
I was fifteen. He came to talk to our school, one of those career talks

Solness
I never did that

Kaja
his path to success, it wasn't just him that day a few professionals came and it was all very interesting

Solness
is anyone actually listening to me?

Kaja
and after I was standing by the bus stop. I don't think I was even thinking about him but

Solness
I never went to a bus stop

Ragnar
they didn't have strawberry ice cream in the first

place, he said if I wanted strawberry then I should
have it, he –

Solness
  this is all lies

Kaja
  as I stood waiting for the bus at the end of the day,
  his car drives right past

Solness
  you know what I now –

Dr Herdal comes on with his own file.

Dr Herdal
  I was with him seven times.

Solness
  what do you want from me?

Kaja
  winds down the window, I think you were in my talk
  weren't you. Didn't know who answer, yes I say

Dr Herdal
  I know because I marked them in my diary

Solness
  I never even met her

Dr Herdal
  I put a heart against every day

Aline picks up a file, and also reads aloud.

Aline
  he was well known in the town. I had just started my
  periods. I had this fight with my dad

Dr Herdal
  he definitely loved me

Solness

this is lies, this is just –

Aline

and I ran out of the house. Mum wasn't there any
more, I couldn't stand it

Solness

you can't believe this, no one would believe this

Dr Herdal

only he said our love wouldn't last, I had to wait until
I was older. And I couldn't tell my mum

Aline

I ran all the way to the train station and sat alone.
I suppose I was waiting for a train or something
but anyway, this man comes up to me, the Master
Builder

Dr Herdal

he was clear about that. Don't tell anyone or I won't
love you any more.

Solness

there's nothing here

Brovik comes out with a file and joins the reading aloud.

Brovik

I saw him three times. No, four. Once was in a hotel.
I didn't mind it actually. I didn't know that there
was anything bad and he was actually kind. When
it hurt he said

Aline

you alright he said

Solness

please stop now

Ragnar
we walked all the way down the street looking for
strawberry ice cream

Dr Herdal
and I kept drawing hearts in my diary.

Brovik
he said he was sorry and it wouldn't hurt again as
much the next time. He said I was beautiful, and
beautiful particularly between my legs and no one
had ever

Dr Herdal
and I sent him a letter too, until he said I wasn't to do
that

Solness
please stop I said

Kaja
get in the car, he said. I'll give you a lift home, you
sure I asked

Aline
yes I am alright I said, well that is good then and
he sat

Brovik
that wasn't a place I thought I was beautiful, so
I didn't mind

Ragnar
it was later that I wondered what he had done.
It kind of made me cry later

Solness
I HEARD IT ALREADY

Aline
down there wasn't a train for an hour, so he bought
me some Fanta

Kaja

I never realised the damage until later. That was the
thing. At the time it was all buzz and excitement

Solness

STOP

Brovik

I was twelve. What was a grown man doing sticking
his hand up the skirt of a twelve-year-old? I was
twelve

Solness

STOP

Ragnar

I have a daughter, she is thirteen. She is thirteen, tiny,
a baby really even if she thinks she isn't

*They all speak their testimony again, this time on top of
one another.*

*The sound of it gets louder and louder until Solness can't
take any more.*

Solness

STOP! STOP STOP. PLEASE STOP. JUST STOP

*He is left standing at the top of the building in silence.
And out of breath.*

Only the sound of his breathing.

alright
alright
I have a troll in me. Is that what you want?

*Solness almost squirms as if he is a snake trying to shed
a skin.*

I have a troll
I have the biggest fucking troll and whatever I do,

or whoever I try to be. He comes up, and he takes
it. He takes it away

He looks at his wife.

I'm so sorry, Aline. I never meant –

Aline
don't –

Solness
you don't understand what it was like trying to live
with it, to be good when all I wanted

Aline
you're talking shit

Solness
I couldn't beat it

Aline
am I supposed to feel sorry for you?

Solness
no

Aline
is that what you want?

Solness
someone should, maybe. It's been torment – you think
please for a second just think –
you think I wanted to be this? It was bigger than me
that's what you have to understand, and everything
I did

Aline
go on then, jump

Beat.

She looks at him and he looks at her.

you want to, don't you? Jump

Solness
   I am sorry

Aline
   jump

He jumps.

Hilde and Aline are left alone. Years have passed.
The light has faded now and it's cold.

Hilde
   you never saw it?

Aline
   it's so long ago now

Beat.

   you ask the same question every time you come
      to visit
   did I, or

Aline
   it's unanswerable. Did I or didn't I?

Hilde
   you never answer

Aline
   I try

Hilde
   you could have saved some of us from some of it

Aline
   only if I knew. Only if I *knew*. Of course I didn't
      know. I suppose that's one part of the answer, I was

so much in my own fog. Can you know and *not* know? I know you don't like that idea either. But I didn't *know* like you know things, like you know good or bad or left or right, I didn't *know* like that. If I knew it was like how you know that something is up with your sister even though you haven't spoken for a while or you remember a word in Greek suddenly out of the blue even though you don't know you knew it. You can know things somewhere and not know them

Beat.

that's all I can say

Hilde
but –

Aline
I've been over and over it, Hilde. Years. That is all I can say. Don't come and see me if you want something more

Beat.

I used to think about things, I know I did, but then I stopped thinking

Beat.

how have you been?

Beat.

how have you been? You come and see me, have a conversation. Your children?

Hilde
the children are good

Aline
you? Your husband

Hilde
husband is fine

Beat.

I am the same

Beat.

Aline
and me the same I guess as well

Beat.

ridiculously. Oh sit down for heaven's sake

Hilde sits down.

why can't we do better? It's gone surely after all
this time. The doctors says hello Mrs Solness, are
you thriving?

Beat.

Hilde
do you ever find you miss him?

Aline
why do you ask that?

Hilde
I don't know, because even after all these years –

Aline
you can't miss him, he was –

Hilde
I realise that, I'm just saying . . .

Beat.

Aline
I don't know why you come and see me. Every year
you make this trek but when you're here

Hilde

    because we are both trapped in it, aren't we? What
      he did, what he made of us and
    we are both in it

Beat.

Aline

    so you do miss him then? In some way

Hilde

    I don't even put the question like that

Beat.

    I wish I could miss him. Maybe it's that. I wish I
      didn't have the taste of him still, the feel of him.
      He will always be on my skin and the fucker,
      wherever he is or whatever hell. He knows it.
    he marked me.

    he is wrapped around, and in and over and on my
      skin and I wish I could get him off

The two women look at each other.

Aline

    me too
    indecent man you don't know what you have done.